Includes DVD featuring leading paranormal experts!

"Nobody digs into the paranormal like Jeff Belanger. Picture Yourself Legend Tripping is a killer way to learn how to explore the unexplained and find the legends creeping in your area."

—Zak Bagans, Host and Lead Investigator for the Travel Channel's Ghost Adventures

PICTURE YOURSELF
Legend Tripping

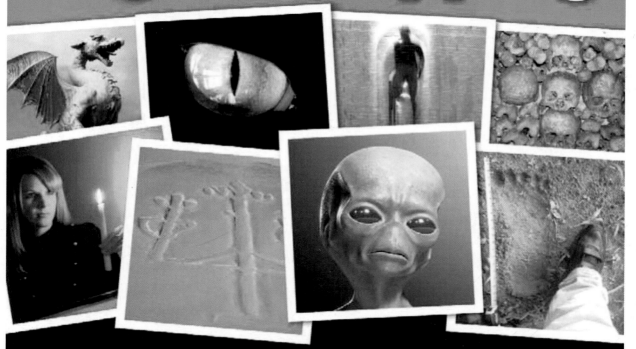

Your Complete Guide to Finding UFOs, Monsters, Ghosts, and Urban Legends in Your Own Backyard

...ger

D1295687

COURSE TECHNOLOGY
CENGAGE Learning™

Picture Yourself Legend Tripping: Your Complete Guide to Finding UFOs, Monsters, Ghosts, and Urban Legends in Your Own Backyard

Jeff Belanger

Publisher and General Manager, Course Technology PTR:
Stacy L. Hiquet

Associate Director of Marketing:
Sarah Panella

Manager of Editorial Services:
Heather Talbot

Marketing Manager:
Jordan Castellani

Acquisitions Editor:
Megan Belanger

Project Editor:
Jenny Davidson

Copy Editor:
Gene Redding

Interior Layout:
Shawn Morningstar

Cover Designer:
Mike Tanamachi

DVD-ROM Producer:
Andrew Lake

Indexer:
Katherine Stimson

Proofreader:
Sandi Wilson

For product information and technology assistance, contact us at

Cengage Learning Customer and Sales Support, 1-800-354-9706

For permission to use material from this text or product, submit all requests online at
cengage.com/permissions

Further permissions questions can be emailed to
permissionrequest@cengage.com

All trademarks are the property of their respective owners.

Library of Congress Control Number: 2010922098

ISBN-13: 978-1-4354-5639-6

ISBN-10: 1-4354-5639-4

Course Technology, a part of Cengage Learning
20 Channel Center Street
Boston, MA 02210
USA

Cengage Learning is a leading provider of customized learning solutions with office locations around the globe, including Singapore, the United Kingdom, Australia, Mexico, Brazil, and Japan. Locate your local office at: **international.cengage.com/region**

Cengage Learning products are represented in Canada by Nelson Education, Ltd.

For your lifelong learning solutions, visit **courseptr.com**
Visit our corporate website at **cengage.com**

Printed in the United States of America
1 2 3 4 5 6 7 12 11 10

For Sarah, Andrew, Matt, and Rob...
Oddballs, friends, and legend trippers one and all.

ACKNOWLEDGMENTS

A LOT OF PEOPLE GAVE A TON of help in formulating the ideas for this book. I've been inspired by so many people that I'd need another book just to thank them all.

Thanks to my fellow Oddballs, legend trippers, and models for many pictures throughout this book and DVD: Sarah Coombs, Andrew Lake, Matt Moniz, and Rob Bailey. Thanks also to Andy White for being part of *30 Odd Minutes* and putting up with our oddness.

There are many investigators, friends, and researchers who have also inspired me, and they're all legend trippers in their own right. Thanks to: Zak Bagans, Nick Groff, Aaron Goodwin, Christopher Balzano, Loren Coleman, Peter Robbins, Nick Redfern, John Horrigan, Jason Lorefice, and Dave Schrader.

Thanks to Mike Scalere for seeing what legend tripping can be and helping to hone the ideas. This book is the foundation. From here we can build.

Special thanks to Normand M. Asselin and Michelle R. Lafontaine for generously supporting the Charles Foley Jr.-Gilmartin Foundation.

Thank you to the folks at Cengage Learning, especially Jenny Davidson for her editorial work, Shawn Morningstar for a great design, and of course thank you to my wife, Megan and daughter Sophie for putting up with the deadlines, the legend trips, and me. I couldn't do this without you!

ABOUT THE AUTHOR

JEFF BELANGER is one of the most visible and prolific legend researchers today. He is the author of a dozen books on the paranormal (published in six languages) including the best sellers: *The World's Most Haunted Places*, *Our Haunted Lives*, *Who's Haunting the White House*, and *Weird Massachusetts*. He's the founder of Ghostvillage.com (the Web's most popular paranormal destination, according to Google.com), and a noted speaker and media personality.

He's also the host of the cable/Web talk show, *30 Odd Minutes*. Belanger has written for newspapers like *The Boston Globe*; he is the series writer and researcher for *Ghost Adventures* on the Travel Channel; and he's been a guest on more than 200 radio and television programs, including The History Channel, The Travel Channel, Living TV (UK), *The Maury Show*, The CBS News *Early Show*, PBS, National Public Radio, The BBC, Australian Radio Network, and *Coast to Coast AM*. He's also the founder of LegendTripping.com—a site devoted to the pursuit of the unexplained. Visit his personal Web site at www.jeffbelanger.com.

DVD-ROM DOWNLOADS

If you purchased an ebook version of this book, and the book had a companion DVD-ROM, we will mail you a copy of the disc. Please send ptrsupplements@cengage.com the title of the book, the ISBN, your name, address, and phone number. Thank you.

Table of Contents

Introduction

"I've looked under chairs
I've looked under tables.
I've tried to find the key
to fifty million fables.
They call me the seeker.
I've been searching low and high.
I won't get to get what I'm after
'Til the day I die."

—The Who

I WISH I COULD TELL YOU THAT GHOSTS are just dead people still hanging around, that UFOs are simply nuts and bolts from a distant, advanced galaxy, and that Bigfoot is an elusive ape that we haven't captured yet, but it's more complex than all of that. There's a reason that you know about certain areas being hotspots for paranormal activity. I know why you might have some trepidation about crossing that old cemetery at midnight when the moon is full, and I know the reason monsters, aliens, and unexplained occurrences won't go away no matter what some people in mainstream science tell us. The reason is: story.

WELCOME TO LEGEND TRIPPING

YOU HEARD A GREAT TALE that stirred your imagination and spoke to your soul, and you felt a genuine connection with the person who relayed this tale to you. You felt compelled to tell others what you heard, and if you've read this far, you're ready for the next bold step—to walk into the legend. To follow tracks, to crawl through dusty, abandoned buildings where tragedy left a mark, and to meet the people who know what they saw and experienced *is* real.

Folklore is about story and oral tradition; paranormal investigation is about trying to apply science to something that can't be measured by our current means; legend tripping is about the experience and adventure. But we're going to take that one step further...we're going to talk about locating these legends, experiencing the unexplained, and documenting your findings.

Some of my essential legend tripping gear ready to go. You probably already have half of this stuff and there's no rush to obtain items like a GPS, survival blankets, ponchos, or video camera. Relax...go legend tripping! (Not pictured, my Nikon SLR camera... I used it to take this photo.)

There's no reason you can't be out there this weekend joining me on an adventure through the woods, through haunted battlefields, or on some hilltop gazing skyward. To fully appreciate the adventure, I ask that you bring your open mind and open heart. Grab your gear, let's go legend tripping.

WHAT WILL I NEED?

No, you don't need thousands of dollars in gear and fancy equipment. You don't need night vision, nor do you need handheld meters that measure electromagnetic forces—that stuff looks cool on TV, but it weighs you down. Bring this:

- ❏ Pen
- ❏ Notebook
- ❏ Backpack (you don't need a briefcase—you're a legend tripper, not a lawyer)
- ❏ Camera (film, digital, video, whatever you have will do)
- ❏ Audio recorder
- ❏ Bug spray
- ❏ Snacks
- ❏ Water
- ❏ Boots
- ❏ First aid kit
- ❏ Extra batteries
- ❏ Some great music for the car ride
- ❏ Your favorite caffeinated drink for those late nights

FOUL !

YOU FOLKLORE INSIDERS MAY recognize the term "legend tripping." You may even be crying foul at how I've defined the concept thus far. *Mea culpa.* Here's how Wikipedia defines legend tripping: "Legend tripping, also known as "ostension," is a name recently bestowed by folklorists and anthropologists on an adolescent practice (containing elements of a rite of passage) in which a usually furtive nocturnal pilgrimage is made to a site which is alleged to have been the scene of some tragic, horrific, and possibly supernatural event or haunting."

That's pretty accurate, but it doesn't say enough. I freely admit I'm stealing the term, broadening the definition, and turning it from a somewhat negative endeavor to a positive. What gives me the right to do this? It's already happening out there in the field anyway—people are seeking legends in a respectful way, and it's not just kids. Plus, I'm the one with the computer keyboard and the book contract. Try and stop me! *Bwahahaha.*

INTERVENTION TIME

THERE IS ONE COMMON thread for people who seek out legends and lore. I'm asking you right here in the beginning of the book to admit it, and own it. You're not above it, and neither am I.

In searching for legends, we want to make ourselves part of the story. Sure, we're trying to be objective, maybe even scientific. Even those people who believe all of this stuff is hooey are still trying to write themselves into the legend.

They want to be the person who explains away something perceived as paranormal and who writes the final chapter of a story. There's no escape. As soon as you walk into any environment, you contaminate and change the place just by being there. Say it with me: *I want to become part of the story!* It's okay. Strive to keep your objectivity because you'll need it. But also recognize that you are becoming part of these legends. As soon as you write down your thoughts and feelings, as soon as you tell friends and co-workers about what you did this past weekend, you are a permanent part of the story. Immortality.

LEGEND TRIPPING AS A HOBBY?

YOU DON'T HAVE TIME FOR A HOBBY

like this? First of all, for me it's a passion. But I recognize that nothing begins as a passion. We dip our toe into a big pool of specialized interest and sometimes find it suits us. I don't expect you to quit your job and join me full-time just yet (the equivalent of doing a cannonball off the high-dive as opposed to just dipping in a foot). But there are so many ways to experience legend tripping while you're doing something else. That's the magic of this endeavor.

I used to work as the marketing director for an international software company. I got to travel quite a bit in the United States and internationally. On these trips there was always time between meetings or at night to see the sights. I chose to go to haunted and mystical locales in some of these cities. I had my camera, a notebook, a pen, and my inquisitive nature to guide me. In many cases I would pre-arrange some of the legend trip visits. For example, touring Paris, France, many people choose to visit Le Louvre. Oh it's a fine museum to be sure, but on my first trip to Paris, I went underground. I heard there were a few million human skeletons below the city that were just dying to meet me. So there I was in the Catacombs.

Je parle un petit peu francais, so I asked around as I got close. People were very helpful. Don't let anyone tell you that the people of France are nasty to foreigners. Just make an effort with their culture and language and you'll go far. I asked where the catacombs were, and an older, matronly woman raised an eyebrow and then brought me around the corner and pointed me toward the entrance. *Merci!*

I've always had a fear of skeletons. Part of legend tripping is to face those fears and embrace the mythos and supernatural qualities of stories and scenes that haunt us. I descended the many spiral cement steps lower and lower into the bowels of the City of Lights. I walked through limestone tunnels covered with graffiti I mostly couldn't read. I made left turns, then right. I'm six feet, two inches tall, and there were plenty of places where I had to duck to continue. Finally I approached a painted doorway that read: *Arrete! C'est ici L'Empire de la Mort*—"Stop! Here is the Empire of the Dead." I took a deep breath and walked through.

I was greeted by six million human skeletons stacked in macabre and intricate patterns all around me.
There were rows of skulls, skulls shaped into crosses, even a valentine heart. Incredible. Dark.
I was walking through 60 generations of Parisians. If these walls could talk.

The Catacombs of Paris, France,
full of skeletons, stories, and
spirits of the past.

Disturbing a place of the dead is a universal taboo, but Paris had no choice. Legend tripping forces you to learn about the past. Centuries ago, the city of Paris placed its cemeteries on the outskirts of the city. Additionally, there was plenty of limestone around for building materials. Over time, workers had to dig to get the limestone, and hundreds of kilometers of tunnels were dug under a city that was growing denser, taller, and heavier. The city had now sprawled and encircled the cemeteries. By the mid-eighteenth century, there was no longer room to bury the dead, so bodies were thrown into rotting piles of corpses. The smell was awful, and the carnage was literally spilling into the streets. But Paris had another problem: The heavy buildings were collapsing into the hollowed-out ground below. The decision was made to empty the cemeteries and seal the tunnels.

The skeletons were brought down and stacked the way they are today. As I walked through close to a mile of this scenery, I realized the only way for these workers to show any kind of respect for the dead was to make this intricate and beautiful pattern. They didn't just throw the bones in a pile. True, we have no way of knowing who was who anymore, but the Catacombs of Paris are indeed a place for the dead and a place for the living to pay their respects. Incidentally, they say the place is haunted.

Maybe people are nervous around so many skeletons, maybe the experience is like psychometry where the living pick up on vibrations of the dead through objects they owned (in this case their bones), or maybe there are ghosts wandering those old tunnels. We'll get to that in Chapter 2, "Ghost Tripping."

LEGEND TRIPPING DON'TS

Don't trespass—always get permission before going to a location. If for no other reason, you may be arrested or shot!

Don't break anything.

Don't take anything away with you other than photos, video, audio, and notes.

Who Is "They"?

They say this place is haunted.
They say if you honk your horn three times at midnight, you'll see the monster under the bridge. *They* say a lot of things. But who is "they"? Grab a mirror and you'll see. They is you, they is me. We are they. Call it the collective unconscious, call it the old telephone game or the power of folklore. We have an inherent need to share powerful stories that speak to us. It's why religious folks feel compelled to give you pamphlets at the airport or knock on your door. It's why people gossip about others. We connect with each other in the telling of tales. Listen to "they," it's a great starting point.

As you begin your own legend tripping adventures, you'll find your connection with your fellow humans will grow deeper and more profound. If you're a shy person, you will get over it if you stick with legend tripping. Being an extrovert is not a requirement, but speaking with people—especially strangers—is. Don't worry, it's not as difficult as you might think, and I'll be with you every step of the way. We're in this together, and if I didn't think you could do this I wouldn't have let you buy this book (of course, I'm kidding—I'd let *anyone* buy this book—daddy needs a new pair of hiking boots, after all).

Sarah just heard a juicy story from Matt. But is it true?

Back to they. Resources for legend tripping are all around you. You probably have a library. Walk in and tell them you're researching local legends.

Rob stumbles across a great book in the library—it's full of leads on local legends.

"What kind of legends?" The librarian may ask as one eyebrow heads north.

"You know… ghosts, monsters, unexplained activity…those kinds of things" is a fair reply.

Librarians live for researching. Honestly. They get excited about finding the right sources for you, in leading you down book-lined avenues. You may find tomes written about your region or state that list all kinds of oddities. Read them! You may be directed to historical societies, archeology clubs, or Web sites. The trick is to ask the right questions.

It's still early in the book, but I'm willing to give away one of legend tripping's biggest secrets. The reason one of your objectives is to document your findings isn't just so you'll have a great diary to read later (though that's a perfectly fine excuse).

> **NOTE**
>
> Approach is everything. The best locations for legend tripping don't have gift shops or offer tours. Many aren't even available to the general public. When you make your initial contact to request permission to investigate, tell them you're documenting this legend. It's a valid reason to get in, and the cause will serve you well.

The reason is: If you have a noble objective such as documenting something, you're significantly more likely to get into a location than someone who just wants a thrill.

When I first started legend tripping, I was writing for newspapers, magazines, and Web sites. Doors open to journalists. I don't care if your day job is as far away from journalism as can be. You can still be a journal*ist*. Start a blog. Film your findings for a documentary. Record audio for a podcast. Write a book. Even if you never intend to publish that book, you can relive your own adventures later in the rereading.

Legend tripping is an adventure. You should savor every thrilling moment, from the research to the field trip to the documentation. Knowing from the beginning you're going to document the experience will heighten your awareness throughout the process. You will be asking the questions: who, what, when, where, why, and how? You'll be taking notes and recording the process. Retelling a great story isn't the only reason to make this documentation effort. You may just find something. If you do, your notes will be invaluable.

This is all about the journey, but if you didn't have a hunch that there might be more to the world than what we're told, you probably would have never thought about legend tripping.

There's something to these stories. Yes, Virginia, there are ghosts and monsters. They've been proven to be real to millions of witnesses all over the world who all trust their senses. You may be the next witness.

START WITH YOURSELF

LOOKING FOR A GREAT LEAD? Begin with your own personal experiences. Almost everyone has had some brush with the unexplained—maybe a prophetic dream, an encounter with a ghost, déjà vu, or a UFO sighting. It's these amazing occurrences that spark fires within us and make us ponder the big questions.

When I was 12 years old, I was living in Newtown, Connecticut. I can tell you with the benefit of somewhat recent research that the date was May 26, 1987. We had a swimming pool in our backyard, and each night in the summer my dad would turn off the pump and lock the gate. It was around 10 p.m., and I was already in bed. I heard my dad screaming in the backyard (my dad is not the screaming-in-the-backyard type, for the record) "Jeff, get out here right now! Hurry! Run!"

I bolted out of bed and ran down the stairs. Seconds later, I opened our back door and asked, "What?!"

"There's a UFO right there, you gotta see this right now!," Dad said.

At that point my shoulders dropped. *Are you kidding me?* I plodded toward him in the backyard. "Dad...seriously, are you kidding...oh...my...God."

"Me?" Yes you, Andrew.

Right there in the sky was a giant circle of lights. It moved very slowly. Minutes went by. Minutes! I heard a low hum. My dad said he saw a beam of light come out from the bottom, but I didn't witness that part. It passed right over our house and then out of sight.

What an incredible event to witness! I hardly slept that night (and I don't think my dad caught too many winks either). The next morning, a front-page story in the *Danbury News-Times* reported that over 100 people had called in about the UFO. The article claimed it was a group of small aircraft pilots who flew in formation and used a rich gas mixture so their airplanes wouldn't make much noise.

Here's the thing. That night there was low cloud cover—not a star to be seen. As this circle of lights passed over our heads, we had no way to know if it was solid or not. If it were a clear night, the stars would have disappeared behind the craft. But it was not. Could it have been a group of small airplanes? Maybe. But then a photo surfaced on the Internet taken by Randy Etting, another resident of Newtown. The picture clearly shows a ring of colored lights—exactly what my dad and I saw that night.

It just doesn't look like a group of small airplanes to me. And there were over 100 witnesses! We didn't all imagine these lights in the sky. None of us were looking for them. I will never be able to explain what I saw, but that event has helped shape me in everything that I do. What an adventure, and I was just a kid about to go to bed!

I was hoping to avoid hunting analogies, but I can't. We are legend hunting. We're putting ourselves where these things happened. The hope, of course, is that lightning will strike twice. That we'll either see an incredible phenomenon or be able to debunk what another witness saw. It is a hunt in many ways, but a hunt where you will come back the overwhelming majority of the time (maybe even every time) without capturing or seeing your quarry. But that's okay, my fellow legend tripper. Your reward is in the journey. It's a journey without end, and I can tell you from almost two decades of experience (so far), it's a wild ride.

I think it's time we get started. Let's go legend tripping!

GHOST TRIPPING

"Why worry? Each one of us is
carrying an unlicensed nuclear
accelerator on his back."

—*Dr. Peter Venkman,* Ghostbusters *(1984)*

I AIN'T AFRAID OF NO GHOST either, which is why I go ghost tripping.
Ghosts are what first hooked me into the weird and wonderful world of
the paranormal. I grew up in an old New England town and had friends
from a young age who believed their centuries-old homes were haunted.
At age 10 I was attending sleepovers at some of the houses with my *Ouija*
board in tow. We would stay up late trying to contact the ghosts who
resided in the house.

What took place all of those years ago was the beginning of my passion for
chasing legends. This was a friend's house—not some Civil War battlefield,
not some creepy abandoned hospital, and certainly not an old graveyard.
Just a 250-year-old house that had seen a lot of history. My friend looked
me square in the eye when he told me he thought his house had a ghost.
When asked, his parents would just sigh (a sigh that said, "Please don't tell
your parents and have us locked up for this") and say, "Yeah, it seems as
though someone else lives here with us, and we see him on occasion."

There was no blood dripping from the walls, no evil possession with heads spinning around, just a great story from credible people I knew who allowed me into their home for dinners and sleepovers. *Wow! You mean I might actually see something if I sleep over?* I was in and hooked by age 10. I wanted to be a part of that story. I wanted to see something and tell others.

I even took out my mom's typewriter, fed in an index card, and typed: "Supernatural Investigator, Jeff" and then listed my parents' phone number. In hindsight this was ridiculous because the only people I gave these cards to already knew me and my phone number. No matter, a career was launched that day.

Turn on your television and turn to a random channel showing a ghost investigation show. There's a good chance you'll be watching people recorded at night in green night-vision cinematography stalking through old buildings or haunted homes in search of ghosts. They have closed-circuit television systems and a host of gadgets that beep, light up, create rainbow-colored imagery of the environment, or record voices of the dead.

If you buy all of the equipment you see on these television shows, you could easily spend $20,000 to $30,000. If those numbers don't faze you, then by all means have at it. But even if you're Donald Trump, I would still tell you that you don't need it. The people and groups you see on those television shows may not even realize it, but they are chasing a story. They heard a haunted legend, and now they're trying to wrap their hands, gear, and gadgets around that legend, trying to prove to themselves or to the world that there's more to the legend than just the story.

The green night-vision view that so many of us have seen on ghost investigation programs.
Photo ©istockphoto.com/George Cairns

I'm not knocking any kind of ghost hunting group. Far from it. My point is that first they heard a story—a story that rang true and stirred something inside of them that made them want to check it out. For some people, just checking it out and speaking with witnesses isn't enough. Those folks want to investigate, document, and record every square inch of the environment. No problem. That's another level, and if you want to go that direction, check out my friend Chris Balzano's book, *Picture Yourself Ghost Hunting*. For ghost tripping, we're going to stick to the story and how to find the haunts.

NOTE

When I ask ghost investigators who have been doing this a long time to tell me their most memorable moment on a hunt, I've never once heard someone say, "This one time we had an EMF spike at the same time the temperature fluctuated three degrees, all while my night-vision camera's batteries instantly drained." The most memorable moments sound more like this: "I saw a full-bodied apparition standing at the end of the hallway. It looked at me, then disappeared." It's always about the experience, not the equipment.

TYPES OF GHOSTLY LEGENDS

THEORIES ABOUND AS TO WHAT exactly *is* a ghost. I've written an entire book that explores that very topic. Here's the most basic definition I can offer: A ghost is a direct connection to our past, a way for living people in the present to bond and speculate, and a ghost is a glimpse at our inevitable future. (We're all going to die—it's one of two guarantees in life. The other guarantee, of course, is taxes.)

Categories of ghostly legends come up. I'm not a categorizing type of person, because I believe every person, every situation, and every "ghost" is unique. However, for the sake of discussion here, I will concede that types start to form when you look at hundreds of these encounters.

PHANTOM HITCHHIKER: This legend goes back centuries, but we think of it as modern because today there is usually an automobile involved. The simplest version of the tale goes something like this: A person is driving along in the cold rain at night when he sees a young woman walking along the side of the road. The driver pulls over to offer assistance. The young woman may even get in the car. As the car pulls away, the passenger disappears.

GRAY/WHITE/GREEN LADIES: These legends are most prominent in the United Kingdom and Ireland, but there are plenty in North America and other parts of the world. Stories are told of seeing a glowing white (or gray or green) female figure wandering (often in a cemetery). Women were traditionally buried in their white wedding dress, so it would follow that their risen ghosts would have that flowing look to them.

HISTORICAL IMPRINTS: You may have heard stories from Gettysburg, Pennsylvania, where tens of thousands were killed or wounded between July 1 and 3, 1863. Today the entire town has a haunted reputation. People report seeing soldiers march across the battlefield and then disappear. It's not likely that a group of spirits collectively decided to get back together for another march on Gettysburg (considering how well it went last time); what's more likely is that it's an historical imprint. For some reason, the witness glimpses an event that took place at that location in the past. You hear similar stories at the sites of murders and other crimes.

FAMILY VISITOR: This occurs when a witness experiences a visitation from a loved one who has passed on. Often there is some kind of message, but mostly the experience itself is comforting, a kind of goodbye. The event is emotionally powerful and doesn't usually repeat.

DISCARNATE SOUL: This is the traditional definition of a ghost. The ghost has distinguishing features, we often give the spirit a name (sometimes a specific name from history if appropriate), and it interacts with witnesses. We speculate that the discarnate soul is still hanging around because he is tending to unfinished business or doesn't realize he is dead.

Stories within all categories make great tales to spin around a campfire. Folklorists believe that when a person retells some ghostly legend, he is drawing from one of these categorical wells and telling a tale. That's true in some cases, but it all falls apart when you have a first-hand witness. We're no longer in the realm of a "friend-of-a-friend"; now it's "*I* saw this."

I enjoy the "friend-of-a-friend" stories as much as the next person, but you'll have my full attention when you say that you witnessed a ghost personally. No matter, though, friend-of-a-friend is a good place to start. Just ask if you can talk to this friend—that will help you judge the validity of the story. (If the teller of tale responds with, "Yeah, well I, err, uhh, lost her number," then maybe you should move on to something else. If you get a name and number, you're that much closer to the real legend and the truth.)

There's a reason that some locations have haunted reputations and others don't. *Something* is happening in the haunts. If a building has a haunted reputation, and people talk about it, then something occurred to birth that legend. If many years go by and no one has any more encounters with a ghost at this location, then eventually people will stop talking about the legend, and it will die. A legend is a living, breathing thing. It's born, it grows, evolves, sleeps, and can die and be gone forever. This is part of the reason why I believe in ghosts and think there's more to it than just stories.

Okay, let's find a haunt and check it out.

FINDING A HAUNT

BECOMING AN EXPERT on your local haunts is easier than you might think. My goal here is to try and take us right up to the point of an invitation to come inside for a legend trip. Let's see how we do.

There are published directories of haunted places (I even wrote one. You can check out: *Encyclopedia of Haunted Places: Ghostly Locales from Around the World* for a listing of several hundred), and there are online listings. To demonstrate how I go about finding a haunt, I asked my three-year-old daughter to point to a map of the United States.

I picked the city closest to her finger to use as our example: Topeka, Kansas. I've never been there and know very little about the place. Good! Let's get started. Because I'm not going to be able to go there for this, I'm going to have to do some remote ghost tripping. My objective is to find a haunt, learn a legend, and find some witnesses to interview. I'll put the whole thing together right here.

Let's start with a Google search.

My daughter points randomly at a United States map.

My first search term is *haunted places in topeka* (no quotes, and Google doesn't recognize capital letters). I decided not to use quotes because first I want to cast a wide net. The first result I got was a Web site I know well: Shadowlands Haunted Places Index—Kansas (www.theshadowlands.net).

As I scroll through the Kansas haunts, I find 11 listings in Topeka. For this search, I'm skipping over any cemetery haunts because they don't interest me very much. Show me almost any cemetery, and I'll show you a place many people think is haunted. It's a place of the dead; people get nervous around such locations, and their minds wander. I'm not saying some of our cemeteries aren't haunted, I'm just saying it's too easy. I want a challenge here—a place you might not expect to be haunted.

Here's one from the Shadowlands Web site: "Topeka—Overland Station—Former ATSF train station reportedly haunted by at least three entities: One is a woman occasionally seen dressed in early 20th century apparel on the second floor of the station, another sighting is of a former ticket-clerk who is often seen at 'his' ticket booth, and a small boy, possibly ten years old, often appears in pictures taken outside the building, as well as in reflections in the windows of the station."

I have a soft spot in my heart for trains and train stations. My grandfather used to have a basement full of old American Flyer toy trains that rumbled his house when he had three or four going at once. Plus, there's something romantic about a train station—and something dangerous. This one spoke to me.

As with many online resources of hauntings, there can be a lot of inaccuracies in these listings. This is no fault of the Web site editor or owner, necessarily. He's passing on the leads that come in from all over. Sometimes the sources make mistakes. But what we have here is a starting point, a nugget of a ghostly legend and a location. Let's start digging into Overland Station in Topeka.

The Web site is easy to find: www.greatoverlandstation.com. The site is full of information about its history. The station opened January 27, 1927, and was operated by the Union Pacific passenger railroad. The last passenger left the station May 2, 1971. The site goes on to report that the building was remodeled into offices and then abandoned in 1988. A fire damaged the structure in 1992, and at that point the building's future looked grim. It was set for demolition, but a local heritage organization set out to try and save the building and turn it into a museum. Union Pacific donated the building to Topeka Railroad Days, Inc., and in June 2004, The Great Overland Station opened its doors once more, this time as a museum and landmark. So we've got a great old building (old by Kansas standards, but not so much by New England standards and certainly a baby by European standards) with a lot of movement and memories.

Every building has a story to tell, but the bigger the building and the more people who passed through its doors, the bigger the story. Legend tripping is all about finding those stories.

I'm hooked now.

Bingo! Exactly what I was looking for—mention of the ghosts from actual news sources. The fourth result is from television station KTKA in Topeka. I click and read the article dated September 21, 2006. The article mentions a Topeka Ghost Tour that guides customers along several stops, the first being Overland Station.

The article has a link to a ghost tour company, but I find it's no longer working. No problem; there's no shortage of ghost tour companies in almost any city. I did another Google search for *ghost tours topeka* and found a Web site called Ghosttoursofkansas.com—the site lists regular tours of downtown Topeka. Time to reach out.

Their Web site has a form only for submitting email, no phone number, so I draft the following email and hit Send:

My next step is to verify that the ghostly legend is discussed in more than one location. If I find this legend mentioned on the Shadowlands Web site and nowhere else, I'm likely to give up on this one and find another location. Back to Google:

> Search for *overland station topeka ghosts* (no quotes because I'm using a sentence fragment).

Dear Ghost Tours of Kansas,

My name is Jeff Belanger, and I'm an author who is currently researching the ghostly legends of Overland Station for a book I'm writing. Is there a person there (such as a guide) I might be able to speak with to quote in my book?

Regards,

Jeff Belanger
www.jeffbelanger.com

Ghost tours are available in almost every city throughout the world.

I also included my phone number. A few words about ghost tours while we wait for a response. Ghost tours are wonderful. If you're in a strange city (I mean strange to you, not just strange in general) and have some time, take a ghost tour. You'll get a local flavor and color you can't get anywhere else. You'll learn some local history and see some places typical tourists never hear about—or you'll hear details about well-known locations that other tourists never find out. (Yes, there's a "but" coming.) *But...* if you take the same ghost tour on different nights from different guides, you'll hear different versions of the same story.

This infuriates hardcore historians and those who try to debunk ghostly legends. Instead of getting angry, how about appreciating the living, breathing definition of folklore in front of you? How about acknowledging what these street-side thespians are attempting to do: bring history and ghost lore to life?

For legend trippers like us, ghost tours offer more of the picture. It's like the view from 20,000 feet —not much detail, but there's something down there. To really legend trip, you'll have to step out of the ghost tour and get inside the haunted buildings. Go alone, or bring a few good friends who are of similar mindset.

The other reason I want to speak with the ghost tour company first is because I hope to find a good approach to contacting the museum itself. I might learn that I should avoid speaking with one manager because he hates the idea of ghostly legends, or that a specific employee has had a profound experience and might be willing to talk about it.

My email works; I receive a reply from Cathy Ramirez, the co-owner of Ghost Tours of Kansas. She agrees to talk to me over the phone about what she knows.

CATHY RAMIREZ: I have collected some stories about Overland Station. Some of the first stories I collected were from Carmen, and he was the night janitor. Carmen believes there was a ghostly ticket taker and the ghostly ticket taker is in the west ticket booth. And the reason he believes it's a ghostly ticket taker is because there were times when he would be tidying up, everything would be in order, but then he'd go back and see drawers would be pulled out, and there'd be papers on the floor shuffled around. One time he had a small table-type fan and he said it was going and it wasn't even plugged in. He also had an old plug-in radio because he liked listening to his music when he was working, and sometimes the radio would come on without it being plugged in.

Okay, great stuff! But this is secondhand (though only one person removed, which isn't too bad in the legend tripping world). Cathy informs me that Carmen is now retired. She also said her ghost tours make a regular stop at Overland Station, and her guests can walk around the outside of the building.

On one tour a photo was taken that she believes shows a ghostly boy with no eyes. They speculate that this boy may have been killed by a train.

I ask Cathy if Overland Station is friendly to ghost people like myself. She mentioned that they haven't been receptive to paranormal investigation in the past, but they aren't opposed to people asking about the haunting. She also mentioned one staff member who isn't receptive at all. I make a note to try to avoid this person when I call. Or if this person is unavoidable, I'll try a different approach. Great information to know!

My next step is to reach out to Overland Station. I'll do this over the phone. Emails can be deleted or ignored. On the phone they have to deal with you. Plus, from a voice they can get a sense that I am who I say I am, that I'm sane (or at least sound that way), and professional.

Let's call and see what happens.

I hear a woman's voice. I tell her I'm researching local haunted legends for a book I'm writing. I'm quickly passed along to another contact. I'm going to leave her name out of this, but I can tell that the subject makes her uncomfortable. As we talk, she tells me that many paranormal investigation groups have requested to come in and check out the place.

This is significant. Many people call her wanting to investigate. This place is haunted. End of discussion. There may not be ghosts there, but it has the reputation. Thus, it's haunted.

She tells me that she doesn't want anyone finding anything because she doesn't want to spook her staff of volunteers. She also said that she's never heard of a visitor asking the staff about the ghosts.

Given that she's already getting phone calls, I would guess that will change soon enough.

Ghost tours regularly stop in front of the building, and sometimes guests look around. But this legend trip will require a ticket in the building. Inside you're free to learn the history, soak up the atmosphere, and talk to the staff. One-on-one, person-to-person, you may just make a connection and hear something they don't say on the regular tour.

I invite you to take it from here, legend trippers. This is exactly how I find and approach a haunted legend. Sometimes these places roll out the red carpet, and in other cases I'm on my own. Most are somewhere in the middle.

EXPERIENCING THE GHOST TRIP

YOU'VE PROBABLY SEEN SOME of the many ghost hunting television shows. You may have even attended a conference or tagged along with a paranormal investigation organization and seen them with a host of electronic gadgets. The picture below always makes me laugh. I took it during a conference/ghost investigation at Waverly Hills Sanatorium in Louisville, Kentucky.

My friends Ron, Nick, Nancy, and I were standing in a circle when I told everyone to huddle in close and hold up their equipment.

After taking this picture, I asked the group to step outside their bodies for a moment. Imagine what we must look like to the outside world? Everyone in the circle got the joke.

There are typically two reactions to this photo:
1.) Non-ghost people usually snicker.
2.) Ghost people usually say something like, "What? No MEL meter?"

The Waverly Hills investigation was amazing for me. I rarely have paranormal experiences, and I'm a guy who has been all over in creepy castles, haunted battlefields, old cemeteries, you name it. But when I walked into this giant abandoned building, something inside of me just said, *whoa.*

A little backstory first. Until the mid-1900s, consumption, or tuberculosis, was often a death sentence. There was little the medical community could do for a person who had the disease except keep him high and dry. Sanatoriums were constructed all over the world—a place where the sick and dying could go to be as comfortable as possible before possibly making enough of a recovery to go home, or passing on.

Waverly Hills was one such sanatorium. The building that we see today was built in 1924 to replace the smaller facility built in 1908. The new building with its gothic architecture was designed to hold 400 patients comfortably. When patients passed away, they took a trip through a tunnel system dubbed the "Body Chute" or "Death Tunnel," so the other patients could avoid witnessing the procession and hearse that came to remove the corpse. In 1961 the building was converted into a geriatric center and then closed permanently in 1980. Thousands of people died inside this building. Today it's considered by many to be one of the most haunted places in the United States.

The "Body Chute" or "Death Tunnel" at Waverly Hills is a 500-foot-long tunnel that was used to discreetly remove thousands of bodies from the sanatorium.

I was surrounded by ghost investigators with thousands of dollars of equipment—thermal imaging cameras, EMF meters, Shack Hacks (radios intentionally broken to scan radio waves at regular intervals), night vision goggles, digital thermometers, audio recorders, every kind of still camera, and enough energy drinks to send a small nation into a diabetic coma.

Don't Get me Wrong

I love my ghost investigation people, but my most profound experiences at Waverly didn't happen via any electronic devices; it happened with my own physical senses.

People who claim to be psychically sensitive will tell you this ability is in all of us. I don't believe in a sixth sense, but I do believe we can naturally extend our existing five. When you turn your lights off at night in your bedroom, you can't see a thing. But wait two to three minutes, and your eyes adjust, your pupils dilate, or open wider to let in more of the limited available light. Likewise, when you're in a quiet environment, tiny hairs in your inner ear extend to pick up subtle sounds, which is why the turning of a page can sound so loud in a silent library, but you don't even hear it on an airplane. Our bodies naturally adjust to pick up on subtleties in an environment. In short...

...we're built for legend tripping!

Waverly Hills Sanatorium in Louisville, Kentucky, today.

I was in the Waverly Hills Sanatorium walking the halls. I had my camera and digital recorder, but I wasn't looking for paranormal photographs or trying to capture spirit voices. I keep those items with me in case there's breaking news. We were on the top of the building in the solarium, where children came to play if they had consumption or if they lived here with an afflicted parent. In the middle of the floor was a baseball. My friend Brendan and I started to tap the ball to each other with our feet—just a gentle push to move the ball four or five feet.

"Come and play with us," I said.

The ball was sitting motionless in the middle of the floor when it suddenly wiggled just a little bit.

"Did you see that?" I asked.

"Yeah, I saw it," Brendan said.

Two other people came over to watch. We continued tapping the ball and asking the unseen force to play with us. After another minute or so, the ball came to a complete stop again, and this time made a half turn on its own.

The top floor of Waverly Hills, where
I played ball with a dead kid.

"Whoa!"

Everyone saw the movement this time. We
continued playing for the next five minutes,
but the event didn't happen again.

Did I just play ball with a dead kid?

Here's the thing… I believe I did. Can I prove it
to you? No. Do you have to believe me? No, you
don't. The legend trip experience was all mine.
But that wasn't the last unexplained event of
the night.

Down on the third floor, Brendan, Nancy, Sheila,
and I had just walked down one wing at the
southwestern end of the building. There were
only two hallways leading down the entire floor,
and the rooms between the hallways didn't have
windows and were wide open. We walked from
the southwestern end of the building to the first
bend, ensuring there were no (living) people
down there. From where we were standing, the
only way into this wing was to walk by us.

The ghost-hunting gadgets were out in full
force. In fact, Brendan has his thermal imaging
camera. His FLIR model is similar to what law
enforcement and fire departments use. The
camera mainly finds heat signatures and turns
them into color—the brighter the color, the
hotter the object. When you point the camera at
a living person, he becomes a rainbow of colors,
and the center part of the body glows almost
white, while the extremities are hues of red
and orange. I was holding the mini monitor and
video recorder, and Brendan pointed the camera
down the hallway.

What's that? Brendan and I clearly saw a glowing
reddish ball making circular patterns maybe
50 feet away from us. We both saw it. What the
heck was that? My pulse started to race. The ball
grew larger and closer and THEN… *flap, flap, flap,
flap*, we both get buzzed by a bat zooming down
the hall.

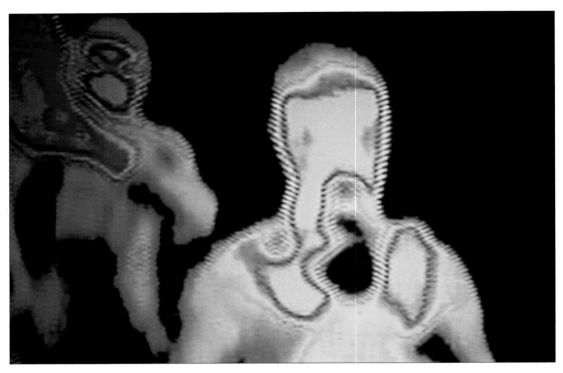

An example of a thermal camera image showing heat signatures of two people.
Photo ©istockphoto.com/David Pedre.

"This camera retails for about $14,000," Brendan says. Brendan Skeen is also the founder of Ghost-Mart, a large online retailer for ghost hunting equipment. "I've never caught anything paranormal with it."

This night was no different. Just a bat. We laughed, because it's okay to laugh when legend tripping. It was late, and we were in an old, abandoned, creepy building looking for ghosts, after all.

But then I saw something down the hall—maybe 20 feet from where we were standing—fourth door down on the left.

"Do you guys see that?" I asked.

One by one the answers came, "Yeah. Fourth door down on the left."

The shadow of a person was standing halfway out of the doorway. There was no fear right then, just a feeling of *Huh, how did someone get by us?* The figure ducked into the room. We immediately walked down the hall to investigate. As we walked, we were able to see through each room to the hallway on the other side, and we reached the fourth room on the left a few seconds after the sighting. Nothing. No one.

And no one got by us, we were still alone. Another sweep of the wing confirmed that. Only then did it sink in. Wow! I may have just seen a ghost! No cameras rolling, no EMF meters spiking at that moment, no psychic mediums channeling Elvis, just an experience—and a big one at that.

I left Waverly Hills very late and invigorated. An experience like that makes me eager to return home and plan my next legend trip.

I took this picture because this is where it happened. To me, it's indisputable.
I don't have the patience to sit here all night clicking in hope of capturing a photographic anomaly.
I had my experience and wanted to document where it happened. The experience itself is my trophy.
This photo serves as a reminder and can take me right back to the moment.

THE VIGIL

MANY OF THE GHOST HUNTING shows on television prominently feature the *vigil* aspect of the hunt. Though the shows don't call it a vigil, that's really what it is: You sit around waiting for something to happen. I'm all for the vigil. Sometimes you just need to shut up and appreciate your surroundings. Smell the haunted roses, if you will.

For me the vigil is more like a walk in the park, as opposed to a hunting trip where you must remain motionless for great periods of time lest you scare your quarry.

Given these two prominent theories, sitting motionless for hours at a stretch may not have any impact on whether you have a personal experience or not. If it's a movie playing over and over, you're going to catch that "movie" or you're not. Moving around might increase your chances of seeing another one.

If the phenomenon *is* intelligent/a discarnate soul, then you have to think of these things in very human terms. If you walked into a room that was familiar to you and you saw a person sitting in the corner holding a bunch of electronic equipment that looked very foreign to you, would you want to walk in and interact?

Or would you be more likely to interact with the person walking around casually, admiring the scenery? What if that person were talking to you as well, saying, "Hello? Anybody here? I'd like to talk to you."

I can't stress enough, when legend tripping, don't be shy and don't be afraid to feel silly. You're here because you heard a compelling ghost story. To fully enjoy the trip, let some inhibitions go.

WHAT IS A GHOST?

I'm trying to avoid theories in this book for the most part, because all any of us can do is speculate as to the cause of these legends, and your speculation is as good as mine. Plus, half of the fun of legend tripping is coming up with your own ideas as to the cause. So please forgive this intrusion, but I do have a point to make.

Two prominent theories about ghosts are that they are either a residual imprint on the environment, meaning there is nothing intelligent or interactive there. It's kind of like a movie that plays itself over and over again, and for some reason some people can tune into the frequency almost like a radio wave.

The second theory is that a ghost is a discarnate soul—a person who died and whose spirit is still hanging around for any number of reasons, including unfinished business, the person doesn't know he's dead, or he's simply stuck in a location for some other reason.

There are many more theories as to what a ghost is, but let's stick with these for now. If you want to dig deeper, please have at it, legend trippers. Take any of these subjects as deep as you wish. Stay up late thinking about them, and read all you can if that's where your trip takes you.

PROVOKING THE SPIRITS

YOU'RE SOMEWHERE, and you believe there might be something unseen lurking nearby. Don't be shy, try to interact! Try saying, "If you're in here, I'd be glad to talk to you or help you if I can." If the legends revolve around ghostly pranksters or children, offer to play a game. Bring a ball to toss, or leave some toys out. Imagine inviting a ghostly child to play with a car and seeing it roll on its own.

Then there's the more confrontational approach, especially if there are dark spirits present—the bygone specters of people who did evil deeds. Some folks will yell at these ghosts, maybe call them by name (if they know it). "Why did you murder those people, you coward?" Others might use religious provocation—reading religious texts, throwing Holy water, or burning a sage smudge to try and force the ghosts into action.

This is one of the more controversial aspects to legend tripping because some people claim to be pushed, scratched, or even possessed by these unseen forces.

By interacting, you are changing the energy of the room. I'm not getting all new-agey on you, I mean you literally alter the atmosphere. Go ahead and try a test: Walk into your living room right now and scream (really scream) in anger. If someone is in the room, he will be startled. But notice how the room feels right after your scream. There's a resonance that will vibrate sometimes for many minutes after. Ever walk into a room where two people have been arguing and you can feel it? Same type of thing.

Don't be shy, but also don't do things that are too far out of your comfort zone. It's legend tripping, have fun!

THE WRITE-UP

THERE ARE ALLEGED HAUNTS in almost every town and village in the world. Some are world renowned because of the media attention they've received, but with the vast majority, you need to get local and talk to people. You need to be respectful. A business card helps because you're offering up your contact information from the start, you're not some thrill seeker or prowler (okay, I admit I'm a thrill seeker, but I can get my thrills in a respectful and legal way).

After your trip, gather your photos and write up your findings. Capture the experience; your experience and the encounters of others. For me, I like to digest for one to two days after my trip before I write everything up. During the trip and even that night, I seem to have too many thoughts and memories going through my head to be able to document. But give me a night to sleep on it, and I find meaning.

Do what works for you, but document your trip. Do it in a blog, or a video log, or an audio podcast recording. Share this incredible experience. And don't forget to have fun with this part. You're now a part of the story, and it's your duty to tell it your way.

So There I Was in Cincinnati

I WAS INVITED TO SPEAK at a paranormal conference at the Cincinnati, Ohio, Music Hall... and they say the place is haunted. What an opportunity to do a little legend tripping during the conference! As with many paranormal conferences, part of the experience is the chance to explore a legendary hot spot with like-minded people.

When I first approach the majestic building, I'm taken in by the architecture. Tyler, who drove me to the place from my hotel, warns me that this is not the best neighborhood. He figures there's a one-in-four chance of something bad happening if I wander too far from the building. There are five police officers stationed around the front of the building, ensuring safety. Glancing around, I figure Tyler is probably telling the truth.

The Cincinnati Music Hall in Ohio. They say it's haunted...

The Cincinnati Music Hall is like an island of beauty and pride in an otherwise crumbling neighborhood. As a legend tripper, it's always nice to speak with neighbors regarding a legend, but I think this time I'll stick to resources inside the building.

I confess, I didn't do any historical prep before arriving at the Music Hall. I was told the place is haunted and that's why the conference is here. Fair enough, I'll do my research on the ground.

I climb the stairs to the hall where the conference is taking place. It's a beautiful room with an arched ceiling. The ghost conference vendors are already setting up. I start to hear talk of why the Music Hall is haunted.

"It's built on a burial ground," one passing voice says. (Yeah, that old one.)

"There used to be a hospital here," another says.

"People see a woman wearing an old-fashioned dress and a bonnet."

Throughout the day, guided tours wander through the building, regaling visitors with tales of the hows and whys behind the building.

To the employees of the Music Hall, this conference is a curiosity. As of this writing, the Cincinnati Music Hall is not an internationally known haunt. It hasn't been featured on any of the ghost investigation television shows.

This is a real legend tripping opportunity, indeed. When a location becomes renowned for haunting, there's a rote to the telling of the ghostly tales by staff. The employees are so used to repeating the legends and even their own personal encounters that there's no life in the story anymore. It's the equivalent of fast food, as opposed to a gourmet meal.

As the sun sets, the group of attendees prepare for a night of looking for ghosts. Throughout the day, I notice the staff of the Music Hall are no longer standing against the wall with a raised eyebrow wondering if we are for real. Now they're coming forward, which is good, because I have questions.

As the group assembles on the third floor of the Corbett Tower, I sit down on the couch in the hallway outside of the main meeting room. I'm chatting with John Kachuba, an author of several paranormal tomes, and we're talking about the job. As the group files out, the two of us are left sitting with a white-haired security guard who is eyeing us from across the room—there's obviously nothing else to watch now that the group has gone.

"Have you seen a ghost here?" I yell over to him.

He smiles, nods, "Oh yeah, I've seen 'em," he says. He gets up and walks over to the empty chair beside us and has a seat. I reach into my bag and grab my audio recorder. I know something great is about to happen.

His name is Charlie, he's had both a heart attack and a quintuple bypass. You can see from the photo on his security badge and from the way he carries himself that he used to be a larger man, and I can tell by his hoarse, wheezing laugh that this man is a character. I can also tell he's glad to have the company and someone interested in what he has to say. I'm instantly grateful I didn't take the group tour. He's worked here 11 years, he says.

For the next 10 minutes, I don't think Kachuba or I spoke more than 20 words or so.

"What happened?" I ask after Charlie helped himself to the seat.

"It's about 2:30 in the morning one time, and this ghost passed me. Down in the lower hall right down here (he points below us). See, this used to be a courtyard that was open one time. So he had to come out of the courtyard and pass me and go in the auditorium (laughs). I couldn't walk, I just froze. My whole back— you can't describe the coldness. You really can't describe the coldness when they walk by you. As soon as he hit the door—those doors are all free swinging' (slaps his hands together)—the door went like that, and I went back to normal (laughs). I went about finishing my work. Naw, I didn't think anything of it (laughs). They don't bother me 'cause I'm taking care of their building.

"Once in a while, I'll aggravate them a little bit. I'll slam a door real hard somewhere (laughs). I'll say, 'well they heard that one' (laughs).

I asked Charlie what else he's experienced in the building, and he starts talking. He wavers between telling us tales of finding water leaks and saving the day, back to ghosts, back to breaking in rookies and showing them how to lock down the building at night, on to how he won't walk in this room over here because they're always moving tables and chairs around, another mention of a ghost, to his flashlight that he doesn't need, to how fast he got back to work after his heart attack, to how well the exercise is keeping him, walking two, three nights a week.

Charlie is legend-tripping gold. Just a few guys talking. We are buddies now, and buddies might share some secrets, like stories other people won't tell or give you access to places others won't allow.

"Everybody's got a story to tell here," Charlie says. He tells us of an electrician who was wiring the ground lights for the chairs in the main auditorium years ago. "He said every morning there's this girl with a long dress and a bonnet on her head would squat down there and watch him. He said it went on for about a week—she was there every morning sittin' there with him. After a few days he got used to it."

There's something to the legends behind the Music Hall, (there usually is, otherwise the legend would not have been born). So begins the research.

The seating area to the side of the stage where there have been ghostly reports.

Some online research shows that in 1821, the state of Ohio established that a hospital and lunatic asylum would be constructed on four acres of land bound by the Miami and Erie Canal. In 1832 a cholera outbreak in the city left hundreds of people dead and many orphans. The facility was converted into an orphan asylum. An 1838 map shows the asylum where the Music Hall now stands. Over time, locals took to calling this building the "pest house," because the facility was used to isolate people with infectious diseases. The grounds around the building became a Potter's Field, a mass graveyard for people too poor to afford burial, or those with no one to claim their mortal remains.

The deceased weren't placed in coffins, just wrapped up and buried in the ground.

These were the homeless, suicide victims, John and Jane Does, and those who meant to just pass through but ended their journey in Cincinnati. Today you wouldn't know it, but in the early 1800s, this was the outskirts of town. By 1857, the city had expanded, and neighborhoods lined the side streets surrounding this now-famous address. In 1859 the property was converted into Elm Street Park, and so it remained until 1876, when the Music Hall Association purchased the land.

There were no headstones, just mass graves, so workers began to dig the foundation. What remains weren't unearthed were simply built over. The Music Hall rose from the ground to become a magnificent structure in only one year.

Over the coming years, expansion projects added on to the building. In 1988 one project involved digging a new elevator shaft. On the first day of digging, 88 pounds of bones were found, and the next day, 119 pounds of bones came out of the ground. Skulls and dozens of leg bones of both adults and children were discovered.

The physical evidence is there: Music Hall literally sits on a foundation of bones. The discovery is in the newspapers and occasionally in the minds of the staff, performers, and patrons. And then little things start to happen. Darting shadows, apparitions, voices. We can't help but look for a reason, a murder, a suicide, some story that compels us to identify the specter with the name of a once-living person, or at least hone in on where and why this ghost might be here.

As I mentioned earlier, I try to avoid large groups when legend tripping. Many people offer many variables and much chance for contamination of the environment. If I know there are only three or four people in the room with me, I can quickly figure out if something I'm seeing is one of us or something unexplained.

In the Cincinnati Music Hall, I wander off with four others. We have the chance to lurk backstage in the dark and sit where the orchestra performs. I sit in a chair by the edge of the stage near where (I think) the violins would be. The main hall is mostly dark, though my eyes quickly adjust as light from the Exit signs and other low-level lights fill the dark void so that some details poke out from the blackness. The chandelier hangs high above like a dark spider perched above an empty audience. The seats become identifiable for what they are—thousands of empty seats.

Jake, who has investigated the Music Hall before, tells us how a little boy was taking a tour with his father one day when he walked up to the box seats that sit near the stage to my right (the far left if you were sitting in the audience facing the stage) and talking to someone no one else could see.

I click a picture of the area—forgive me, it's dark in there. While I'm on stage, someone else reports seeing a darting figure backstage. So I walk back to see.

The backstage is darker than the front, but just as interesting. I wait. I listen. Nothing. But it's late, it's dark, I'm with good people and seeing a side of the Cincinnati Music Hall that very few get to see. With the exception of security and some staff members, not even employees or actors get to be here this late when it's this dark and quiet. Just a few of us legend trippers, and the ghosts, wherever they may be.

Ghostly lore calls to us because it is often a connection to our past. If we can just see them, touch them, hear them, or experience them in some way, we get validation that there's something more out there waiting for us in the universe. The history (be it tragic or otherwise) sets the stage, and the ghosts perform—but never on cue. That's why we take ghost trips—we hope for the off chance that tonight will be the night they decide to show up and make us a part of their legend.

Backstage at the Cincinnati Music Hall. Someone saw a shadow figure move back here just a few minutes before this picture was taken.

Children's
Legend Tripping

"Cross my heart and hope to die
Drop down dead if I tell a lie."

—Children's nursery rhyme

YES, VIRGINIA, THERE *IS* A SANTA CLAUS. Who can blame us for our love of legends, considering they've been indoctrinated into us from such a young age? Even if we were raised by non-religious parents, we still heard about Santa Claus, the Tooth Fairy, and the boogeyman, among other creatures with magic powers. We were taught to believe in them, and we were told what they look like and what powers they possess. We altered our behavior because of them. These people and legends are indisputably real.

Add to that the rituals and supernatural practices such as spitting in your hand before shaking on something, or crossing your heart, just two demonstrations of how kids embrace lore.

Those legend trippers with children in their lives will find no shortage of material for pursuit. Interviewing kids, adults with childhood memories of those legends, or the people who portrayed those characters as adults all have insight into the legends that are still alive and well and continue to evolve as each new generation molds them.

In this chapter we're going to find the legends from our own childhood, prove they're real, and find new creatures from the world of children.

SANTA CLAUS

I CAN PROVE SANTA IS REAL using this page of this very book. It will only take a minute. Walk into a crowd anywhere —your office, a restaurant, a family picnic, it doesn't really matter. Hold up the picture on this page showing the big guy with the white beard and red suit and ask people one simple question: "Who is this?"

Unless someone is messing around with you, I'm willing to bet you a beer that 99 out of 100 people will easily identify the image as Santa Claus. It doesn't matter if they believe there's a house at the North Pole full of elves making toys, they know the image. Many even know pieces of Santa's backstory. Like many great legends, Santa has a base in fact.

Nicholas lived in the land of Myra (modern-day Turkey) around 300 AD. He was the only child of a wealthy family and was orphaned at a young age. The boy grew up in a monastery and entered priesthood by age 17. He gave away his wealth throughout his life. He left gifts for children in their shoes, and he was known to toss small sacks of gold through open windows and to lavish affection upon the poor. The Catholic Church canonized him after his death, and his spirit of generosity was soon incorporated into the Christmas holiday, which the church placed on December 25. Over the centuries, his story was passed around, and he was copy-catted before his legend grew to mythic proportions and took on supernatural attributes.

The first time a child meets Santa Claus, it's like meeting the world's biggest celebrity. Most of us never forget the racing heartbeats, the giddy excitement, and maybe even the fear of meeting this omniscient, supernatural being who can either make your dreams come true by laying your most desired toy under the Christmas tree or crush you with lumps of coal in your stocking.

As we get older, our ideas of Santa morph and evolve until many of us actually become Father Christmas—either at the office holiday party or when we have children of our own. The Santa experience offers genuine miracles on both sides of the fluffy white beard in a world where most mysteries are dying off at an alarming rate.

Since Santa went mainstream in the nineteenth century, he's has been deified, lampooned, imitated, commercialized, scorned, and overexposed. But through all the murk and mess, Santa's magic still shines through like Rudolph's nose in the fiercest blizzard. We teach our own children about Santa because, even if only for the first few years, it's right to believe in magic.

Do you remember thinking you heard footsteps on your rooftop? Or did a red, glowing light in the night sky on Christmas Eve make you think that it was certainly Rudolph leading Kris Kringle's sleigh team and not an airplane? Did your parents use Santa for extortion to get you to behave better—at least in December? Remember when your Uncle Larry, who dressed up as Santa, had way too many hot toddies and crushed the Christmas tree?

Santa is more than an institution. The United States Post Office takes in his mail during December; shopping malls around the world employ him; large corporations such as Coca-Cola use his image to shill their products. How can anyone possibly argue he's not real?

Grab your recording gear, legend trippers. We're going to document a holiday legend that's bigger than big. There's much to learn from interviewing all involved regarding Old Saint Nick.

Anyone who has ever survived Christmas has a Santa story to tell. For more insight on Mr. Claus, I reached out to the big man himself… well, sort of. I reached out to a guy I used to work with who got to don the red suit each December for an annual holiday party where employees brought in their young children. Howie Adams is 65 years old and working in Westport, Connecticut; I had only one question: "What's it like playing Santa at the office party?" What follows is a transcript of the conversation:

It's great with the kids, with the looks on their faces and everything. They just love it. It's like I'm a god. This is it. This is the man they look up to, and they really worship, and they really wanna get all the goodies for Christmas. You know what I mean?

They finally bought me a real suit. Last year they gave me this total piece of shit—I said, "You expect me to wear this?" I said, "It looks like I'm Salvation Army, I am not wearing this." So they bought me a real good one. I have it in my closet at home.

My granddaughter, she was two last year. You'd think she would recognize the voice and everything, but she was mystified by the whole bit, the whole outfit. Some of them cry—they're scared because they're young, you know. Some of the older ones, they see me every year, they're getting older and they're starting to figure it out. They don't say too much, they don't squeal on ya, pull your beard off or somethin'. With some of them I say, "You say anything, you'll get a good swift kick in the butt for Christmas, kid. Don't you mention it to your little sister."

Howie is a real character—ex-cop, born and raised in New York City. His perspective is funny. He'sa rock star. For others, an experience as Father Christmas is more touching. Several years ago I interviewed my friend Dave Gotcher, who was 36 years old at the time and living in Dallas, Texas. He told me about an experience he had while living and working in California. He said:

I played Santa at Universal Studios Hollywood for five years. Parade, lap, and media Santa. But my favorite memory as a Santa was when I went out with a group of volunteer performers to a place that was basically a day care center for senior citizens who couldn't really take care of themselves. That's where I met Frank. Frank had a stroke and couldn't speak anymore. A nurse/helper-type person wheeled him up to me and said, "Frank, tell Santa what you want." I watched as this man who reminded me of Kirk Douglas struggled to try to speak, and I saw the tears build in his eyes when he couldn't, and I heard myself say, "It's all right, Frank. Santa never forgets a friend, and we go way back. I know what you want and I'll do my best. Bless you Frank." I'd never said bless you to anyone before. Frank then grabbed me in a hug so tight I thought my ribs would break. We were both crying openly. Absolutely no shame. As we were leaving, the nurse said Frank had been unresponsive for a week before that visit. I went back the next year, and all they knew was that Frank was no longer there. I sure hope he got that wish.

The legend of Santa is revisited every December whether we like it or not. As legend trippers, we have a unique opportunity. There are very few legends that appear with such frequency and at a specific time. Each season brings the opportunity to document a new aspect of this legend: pen an article for your local paper full of interviews with children who still believe; don the big red suit and white beard one year and walk a mile in Papa Noel's shoes, documenting the reactions you encounter; sit around with the old timers and chronicle their earliest Santa memories. The possibilities are endless, the endeavor is both satisfying and fulfilling, and you may just catch your own Christmas miracle.

Tooth Fairy

GROWING UP IS DIFFICULT for kids. There are so many emotional and physical changes happening to our bodies, it's a wonder any of us survives to adulthood. Losing your baby teeth can be a traumatic event. It's like losing a physical piece of yourself, but it's also a rite of passage. As with any rite of passage, there are varying traditions around the world to deal with it.

Many cultures believe in witchcraft and folk magic, and one way to inflict harm on someone from a distance is to obtain a piece of his body: some strands of hair, a piece of fingernail, or a tooth. In some cultures, teeth had to be disposed of properly to ensure the person wouldn't become the victim of bad magic. He might throw the tooth over the roof or bury it deep in the ground to ensure it doesn't fall into the hands of someone with bad intentions.

When a child's tooth is lost, they say a fairy will soon visit.

Another tooth-disposal option was to feed the lost tooth to an animal such as a rat or mouse. The belief was that if the mouse eats the tooth, the child's new adult teeth will grow to be sharp and strong. The mouse is the key to the origins of this childhood legend.

A French children's fairytale called "La Bonne Petite Souris" (The Good Little Mouse), written by Marie Catherine d'Aulnoy in 1697, has been passed around and translated for centuries. Though today it's an obscure tale, it would appear to be the origins of the Tooth Fairy. In the story there are two kingdoms: a Joyous Kingdom and a Tearful Kingdom. The Tearful King was cruel and jealous of the Joyous King, so he set out to wage war. The Joyous King lost the battle, and his queen and her unborn child were taken as prisoners.

In many parts of the world, the Tooth Fairy is depicted as a mouse.

The Tearful King decided he would spare the captured queen's life if she gave birth to a daughter who might make a suitable wife for his son. The Joyous Queen was imprisoned in a high castle turret and fed only three peas and a scrap of black bread per day. The only bright spot to her day was from a little mouse that came to visit. Though the Queen had very little, she offered the mouse one of her peas. With a puff of magic a full plate of food appeared before the Queen.

Soon the mouse revealed herself to be a fairy in disguise who was so touched by the Queen's act of kindness that she agreed to help the Queen and her daughter escape. Treachery ensued as another jealous fairy abducted the baby princess, but the mouse fairy was still able to save the now-doomed Queen from hanging. In a final battle, the mouse fairy hid under the Tearful King's pillow and waited for him to fall asleep before she sneaked out and gnawed his ears until they bled. The king cried out, but he couldn't figure out how this happened.

Again the mouse attacked and gnawed the King's nose, eyes, mouth, tongue, and teeth. When the Tearful King's son charged in the room, he too was attacked, and soon the King and son fell on each other's swords, ending their reign of terror.

Gruesome, huh? In Spanish-speaking countries, the Tooth Fairy is known as "El Ratoncito Perez" (the tooth mouse), in Italy, "Topino" is the name for the Tooth Mouse, in French-speaking countries it's La Petite Souris Depuis (the little tooth mouse), and in English-speaking countries, she's simply the "Tooth Fairy."

Many people in North America have forgotten the rodent roots of this rite-of-passage fairy. Here's your legend-tripping assignment (hopefully you live in a neighborhood with some ethnic diversity): Talk to your neighbors with children and ask them to tell you the story of the Tooth Fairy that they tell their children. When conducting this research, it's critical not to lead the interview subject (see Chapter 7, "Interviewing the Witness").

Ask high-level, simple questions first:

▶ "Do you have any special traditions for when your child loses a baby tooth? If so, what do you do?" Try to avoid using the term "Tooth Fairy." You may be surprised at a name or tradition you've never heard before.

▶ "What does your child think of this tradition? Does it ever frighten him? Does he anticipate this event?"

▶ "How has it helped or hurt your child through the tooth-loss process?"

If you can also interview the child, all the better. Let your recorder roll!

EASTER BUNNY

HOLIDAYS ARE FILLED WITH LEGENDS and supernatural creatures, and Easter is no different. The origins of the Easter Bunny are pretty obvious: fertility. Let's look at the prominent symbols. The rabbit is known for its reproductive prowess (and for giving birth to large litters in the spring). And if that image isn't enough, society combined it with the egg. If combining a rabbit symbol with an egg symbol doesn't drive the point home that this is about the kind of lovin' that leads to babies, the holiday takes places in the Spring when the sun warms things up and new life and color breaks forth from the flora and fauna all around us.

The rabbit and the egg are two common symbols of procreation.

"Ostara" (1901) by Johannes Gehrts. The goddess Ostara flies through the heavens while Germanic people look up at the goddess from below.

Even the name of the holiday, Easter, is a derivative of the goddess of fertility, Ostra. The holiday was most commonly celebrated on the vernal equinox to celebrate the first day of Spring. Easter is also a reference to the direction "east," the rising sun, and the daybreak season of the year.

The Easter Bunny tradition has its roots in 1600s Germany. Good children would take their bonnets and hats the night before Easter, put them upside-down and build bright-colored nests, then hide the baskets in their homes. If they were good children, in the morning they would find colored eggs in their baskets.

My brain suddenly fast-forwarded to after this book is published, and I got a vision of the angry emails I will receive for this section. I'm already three paragraphs into the Easter Bunny and haven't mentioned the resurrection of Jesus. Christians celebrate Easter to commemorate the resurrection of Jesus Christ. It's *the* most important Christian holiday because it fulfills their savior's promise to return from the dead and prove that he is the son of God. In the Bible (Exodus 12:1–17) we learn that Jesus was said to have died and been resurrected during Passover and the Feast of Unleaven Bread. This festival always took place in the early Spring.

In 325 AD., the Council of Nicaea established a formula for setting Easter's date. The general rule is that the holiday should be celebrated on the Sunday following the first full moon after the Spring equinox (as early as March 22 or as late as April 25).

Easter also marks the end of Lent, a 40-day period of fasting and personal sacrifice for Catholics. In some traditions, Catholics were told to abstain from eggs during Lent, so Easter Sunday also welcomed the return of eggs for families. Eggs were often colored red to signify the renewal of life in the Spring, but later to commemorate the blood of Christ's sacrifice.

While the Easter Bunny is a Pagan tradition, the church learned to incorporate its symbols into their belief system in order to make the religion more familiar and comfortable to the masses they wished to convert. We need to remember that literacy rates in the world before the twentieth century were very low. The masses could not read, but they knew their symbols.

Today the Easter Bunny endures with songs, presents, and symbols visible all around us. Though Pagan in origin, he's gone mainstream and seems to be in no danger of going away. Even non-Christian parents can embrace the secular nature of this bunny.

Here's your assignment: Chronicle how you, your family, and your neighbors propagate this legend. The Easter Bunny continues to evolve as new generations embrace him. Write his story now because it will be different in 10 years, 20 years, and so on.

The modern-day image of the Easter Bunny.

BOOGEYMAN

THE BOOGEYMAN IS THE MOST fearsome of all childhood monsters. Why? Because there is no set description of this horrible creature. He is simply the worst creature our individual imaginations can dream up. His description not only varies from region to region, but from house to house on the same street. In some locales, it's the hand of the boogeyman scratching at your window at night; in other places, he's a shapeless mass of pure evil sent to frighten children.

If you doubt his (or her) existence, tell that to any child who ever woke up in the night screaming and crying in terror. The child knows this was no dream—the figure was as real as mommy or daddy.

Those legend trippers who take a paranormal tack to what they do might believe that children are more susceptible to demonic attack, or maybe this is an example of Old Hag Syndrome—a phenomenon reported around the world wherein a creature attacks prone sleepers in the night. For doubters that the boogeyman is real, consider this: there's a word for him. When you tell someone it was a "boogeyman," people know what you mean. Not only that, when you mention the word, the person you're talking to will instantly conjure his own version of the monster.

I posted a request on my Facebook page asking people to describe their childhood boogeyman. As expected, I got quite a diverse list. Here's a few:

- ▶ "A big, ugly, moving Teddy Bear that stayed in my closet."

- ▶ "A big gentle, furry monster with knuckles that dragged on the floor. He was my best friend when I was three, and I couldn't leave home without him. He was very real to me but dissipated after everyone convinced me he was 'imaginary.'"

- ▶ "Deformed children. Just thinking of it still creeps me out!"

- ▶ "A clown!"

- ▶ "I called him 'The Orange-Glitter Man.' His body was covered in, like, some sort of metallic orange paint. CREEPSville."

- ▶ "Sort of just a corpse-y, gross person with werewolf/hairy arms… no idea why, but there it is."

Here's your legend-tripping assignment: Ask your friends and colleagues what their childhood boogeyman looked like. Document these descriptions and then ask about adulthood fears. Is there a correlation? Do they suffer night terrors? Could the early childhood encounters have been so traumatic they stay with the person? Happy hunting, legend trippers. The boogeyman is out there waiting to be found.

SANDMAN

IF YOU LISTEN TO 1950S rock 'n' roll, then you have a warped image of the Sandman, the creature who brings dreams to children each night. In 1954, The Chordettes hit number 1 with their song, "Mr. Sandman." Remember that bubble gum pop classic? "Mr. Sandman (Yes?) / bring me a dream / Make him the cutest that I've ever seen / Give him two lips like roses and clover / Then tell him that his lonesome nights are over." Then in 1963, Roy Orbison released his song "In Dreams," which began "A candy-colored clown they call the sandman / Tiptoes to my room every night / Just to sprinkle stardust and to whisper / Go to sleep, everything is all right."

Parents would tell their children the sweet and kind Sandman would come to their rooms and sprinkle stardust or moon dust onto their sleeping heads to bring them good dreams, but that isn't how the Sandman story began.

Sleeping children would often awake to find "sand" in the corners of their eyes, so they knew the Sandman had paid a visit.

Fortunately, there was one musical group who got near the mark with a song about this dream-bringing legend. In 1991, Metallica had a hit with "Enter Sandman." The song spent 20 weeks on the *Billboard* charts and told of tucking a child into bed for an evening of nightmares, no doubt a nod to the original legend of the Sandman, which began in Germany.

In 1817, Ernst T.W. Hoffmann wrote the short story "Der Sandmann." Here's the Sandman's original description:

"Oh! He's a wicked man, who comes to little children when they won't go to bed and throws handfuls of sand in their eyes, so that they jump out of their heads all bloody; and he puts them into a bag and takes them to the half-moon as food for his little ones; and they sit there in the nest and have hooked beaks like owls, and they pick naughty little boys' and girls' eyes out with them."

It was traditional, especially in the Germanic region of Europe, to use children's bedtime stories as a way to frighten them into behaving better—to scare them into submission to the benefit of the parents. Children were told the "grit" in the corners of their eyes in the morning was actually a little leftover sand from the Sandman—physical proof that the legend is real!

LITTLE PEOPLE IMBIBED WITH MAGIC

WE TELL OUR CHILDREN ABOUT IMPS, fairies, or leprechauns because we heard the stories as kids ourselves. These creatures can be scapegoats for when something breaks, or they can be practical jokers, or they might be lurking in your closet. What I find so fascinating about this category of creatures is that legends from cultures who had no contact with each other describe the same thing. Though they have different names, the descriptions are the same: a miniature human-like entity with magic powers.

Most of us have heard of the Irish Leprechaun, but the Inuit people of Alaska and the Arctic Circle have something they call "Little People." The Wampanoag Native Americans of eastern Massachusetts speak of the pukwudgies. In these cultures, the little creatures are pranksters, possibly even deadly, in the case of pukwudgies.

The Leprechaun is first mentioned in an Irish tale called *Adventures of Fergus son of Léti.* In the story, the King of Ulster falls asleep and is abducted by three lúchorpáin. When the king realizes what is happening, he turns and captures the fairies, who each grant him a wish in exchange for freedom.

Though the Leprechaun is the best-known version of this creature, a similar legend pops up all over the world from cultures that had no contact with each other.

What makes the leprechaun different than other creatures children hear about is that these creatures are neither good nor evil. They're self-serving pranksters, and they can be tricked into granting a wish, but otherwise they prefer to go about their business, not paying much attention to the world of humans. They guard treasures and they can appear and disappear. Pukwudgies can shape-shift into other creatures, and they show up all over the world. Do we need further proof that this legend has a solid base in reality?

Today there are still people who claim to see pukwudgies flitting around in the forest. Modern-day eyewitness accounts pop up in New England, Indiana, and California.

It would seem that the more we pay attention, the more they show up, as if talking about them and posting their names on Web sites gives them power.

You legend trippers have an opportunity to get on the trail of these creatures. Imagine capturing evidence of their existence, gathering more first-hand accounts, and swimming through millennia of Native American lore. If this creature is real, then what else? *That* is the implication with almost every legend we chase. If this is real, what else is?

FICTION? FACT? REALITY? A CONVERSATION WITH CHILDREN'S BOOK AUTHOR Q. L. PEARCE

FOR SOME PERSPECTIVE ON CHILDREN and legends, I reached out to children's book author Q. L. Pearce. She's penned over 100 books for young readers, including eight collections of scary stories. Pearce is passionate when it comes to the value of scary stories for kids. When asked what credentials qualify her as an expert in this area, she replies, "I was a child once. That was very scary."

Q.L. Pearce: All of these stories are part of our human experience. That's how we connect from one generation to the next.

You tell your children that Santa Claus is real, you do the whole thing—putting out the milk and cookies—and then as they get older that shifts, and then the time comes when they have their children, and it's repeated on the next generation—that whole cultural thing keeps cycling and cycling and cycling through.

We use legends to teach [kids] lessons. Connect them with your own life—when I was a child I used to do this and your grandma would do that... These stories are a part of this wonderful matrix. We as full-blown adults spring out of our time spent in that matrix.

Why do children need scary stories and frightening legends?

There are a lot of purposes. A parent can use them as a way to keep a child in bed, because you don't want them climbing out the window, and as long as they're convinced that there's some sort of boogeyman or some ghostly creature or something that's a danger to them, that bed is the safest place they can be. What a wonderful thing for a parent. The parent scares the child almost to make them behave.

I don't feel that using the boogeyman is an unfair thing that parents do. I think it's just another tool until your children have that whole self-preservation thing developed. It's a way to keep them safe. But the other thing—imagination is so wonderful, and the kids who are imaginative, they're more creative and they can also relate more to how other people feel. Things like the boogeyman, those are dangers, and if kids can imagine what they might do, they're better off. I've heard about children who create traps for the boogeyman, or they'll put something in front of the closet door, or they'll build something so that the boogeyman can't get them. How creative is that? So they're preparing themselves for whatever they might do if they ran into the boogeyman out in the street.

Fantasy itself is really, really good for kids, whether it be Santa and the Tooth Fairy, or whether it be the boogeyman, because children can use it as a coping mechanism. If kids can run through it in their head, and know what they're going to do, that can relieve stress.

Maybe it's a little misleading to say Santa is a chubby guy in a red suit, but there's no harm done. That's why most kids, when they find out Santa isn't real, they don't feel betrayed for the most part.

Some of these legends continue on because we want to perpetrate them, we want to keep them going. As a child, let's say you're the elder brother out of a family of four, and you eventually don't believe in Santa Claus anymore. Your parents are going to say, "Come on, don't tell the little ones." And you may even join in with the whole thing. You may go down and eat the cookies and drink the milk so the little ones will still believe, and that in itself is a rite of passage because you become the adult by this change in how you feel about the legend.

Pearce asks if I've heard of the Candy Witch, and I have not. Could I have missed some legend growing up? She explains how a new legend was needed to help with a modern problem: childhood obesity and tooth decay. She directs me to an article in the *Wall Street Journal*.

CANDY WITCH

IN 2004, THE JOURNAL *Developmental Science* published a report in which psychologists Dr. Jacqueline Woolley and her group, Children's Research Laboratory, conducted a series of studies on young children regarding their belief in Santa Claus, the Tooth Fairy, Garbage Men (yes, the people who come to collect your trash from the curb each week), and a newly formed character they dubbed the Candy Witch. The Candy Witch visits children on Halloween night and replaces their candy offering with toys for kids—the idea being to get rid of the candy that's bad for the kids and replace it with a toy that won't rot their teeth.

How interesting that she included the garbage man! In a child's eyes, the garbage leaves the house and doesn't come back. It's mysteriously picked up and vanishes. Some children never see the actual process, maybe because their garbage collectors come early in the morning while everyone is sleeping. Why wouldn't the garbage collector become a mystical being to a kid? The study of a group of three-year-olds found that 70% believed Santa Claus to be real, and 78% believed garbage men to be real. That's not much of a difference, statistically speaking.

Dr. Woolley and her group went to preschools and introduced the Candy Witch to 44 children. The group even had a drawing of this witch for reference. Many of the children's parents agreed to play along and replace their kids' Halloween candy with a toy. Given this "tangible" evidence of reality, the kids quickly bought into the concept of the Candy Witch.

Belief makes a *thing* real. Could Dr. Woolley have inadvertently created a tulpa—a thoughtform, something that may have begun as imagination but was brought into reality? (See Chapter 11, "Conclusion," for more on tulpas.) Maybe the "imaginary friends" of our children aren't so imaginary.

Dr. Woolley's study goes on to show the correlation between a child's imagination and advanced social and problem-solving abilities.

The imaginary friend is real—and in legend tripping we must start at that assumption. The debate can begin on whether it's in the mind, the ether, or the world, but the legend is real—especially for children who are not only trying to figure out the world, but who don't know what *not* to believe yet. Maybe adults don't see the boogeyman anymore because of years of conditioning, of being told he's not real to the point where we forgot about him. Thankfully for the boogeyman, there's always a fresh crop of children being born who continue to believe in him and give him power.

The Candy Witch promises to replace calorie-filled and cavity-causing sweets with toys.

Tsk Tsk, Be Gone!

THE IDEA OF EMPOWERING CHILDREN with supernatural powers is a concept that hits home for me. When my daughter was turning three years old, she began fearing things that I couldn't see. I won't say she was fearing things from her imagination because number one, I don't know if it's something only she can see and I can't, or if it is something manufactured in her mind—either way, it really doesn't matter because *she* perceives this scary thing, and her fear of it is 100% real. My wife taught my daughter to hold out two fingers like a peace sign, but parallel to the ground, point those fingers at whatever is scaring her, and say, "*Tsk tsk*, be gone!"

Cute, right? It has ritual to it, and if my daughter believes hard enough, using it vanquishes her fear. This specific idea is borrowed from Joanne Harris's 2000 book, *Chocolat*. Of course this has backfired when it's time to go to bed and she wants to keep playing. I tell my daughter that "*Tsk tsk*, be gone" doesn't work on daddy.

Given how open our children are to legends, what a great family activity legend tripping can be! The physical act of searching for these creatures allows your kids to ponder and ask big questions. Of course not all legend trips are appropriate for kids, so always use your judgment.

No, adult legend trippers, you can't go back to childhood. But given the cacophony of stories we're told and often experience as children, it's small wonder that many of us have a solid foundation in legends and lore. Combine these stories with a religious upbringing, and you have an adult programmed to embrace legend. I can't stress enough how real all of these things are. They exist in the world with us. They can be searched for and found (and often in the least likely of places).

When children are empowered, they can "magic" away what frightens them.

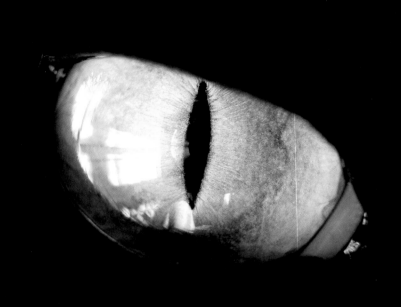

Monster
Tripping

*"We create monsters and
then we can't control them."*

—*Joel Coen, filmmaker*

"MONSTER" IS HARDLY A SCIENTIFIC TERM. It's not a very descriptive word, either. The mention of "monster" conjures up images of a creature that isn't human and is deadly. By that loose definition, there are plenty of creatures we know about that could be labeled a monster: a bear, a shark, a lion—find yourself on the angry end of them, and you know what a monster looks like. We label our mass murderers and serial rapists "monsters," which also seems fair, considering they don't act human and probably don't deserve to be treated like one. What about those creatures that mainstream science hasn't categorized yet, creatures that may (if you believe the tales) have supernatural abilities?

Grab an extra pair of pants for this one. We're going monster tripping.

CRYPTOZOOLOGY

THE FIELD OF CRYPTOZOOLOGY has existed at least since 1892, when Anthonie Cornelis Oudemans conducted a study called "The Great Sea Serpent." Oudemans believed that legendary creatures such as the giant sea serpent should be considered and studied with the same rigor as any other field of biology, except perhaps that the pursuit requires more of an open mind. Oudemans recognized that sometimes sailors made bold claims that were dismissed by marine biologists because what was described didn't fall into their understanding of what sea creatures were out there swimming in the oceans.

By the second half of the twentieth century, cryptozoology was starting to get some legs, as more researchers realized there was a gap between traditional biologists and folklorists. For as long as people have been sitting around fires, people have been coming forward with tales of monsters and bizarre beasts. In the Middle Ages, dragons were the rage. Imagine walking along in the Middle Ages and finding the exposed skeleton of a pterodactyl. Not having an understanding of fossilization, you might assume these bones to be only a few months old. Surely there must be dragons in the area! Physical evidence tied to a legend is a force behind the story, but cryptozoologists are better armed than those wizards and knights of medieval times.

Today, cryptozoologists search for animals that fall into the legend or the thought-to-be-extinct categories or are otherwise nonexistent to mainstream biology. The usual suspects include Bigfoot, the Chupacabra, and the Loch Ness Monster, to name three; however, cryptozoologists have their success stories as well. They include:

The Mega Mouth Shark: Thought to be a legend until discovered and documented off of Oahu, Hawaii, in 1976.

The Coelacanth belongs to one of the oldest lineages of fish in the world. Fossil records indicate this species developed around 400 million years ago but then disappeared 65 million years ago. Biologists labeled this fish long extinct. But then it turned up in a fisherman's net in 1938 off the coast of South Africa.

Mountain Gorilla: Thought to be an East African myth until October 1902, when Captain Robert von Beringe shot two of them.

Giant Squid/Architeuthis: Thought to be the stuff of Jules Verne novels—squids just didn't grow to be more than 40 feet in length. But in the late 1800s, dead giant squid occasionally washed up on shore or landed in the net of a fishing boat and made the news. It wasn't until 2004 that a giant squid was actually photographed alive and well in the wild.

It defies logic why some so-called skeptics shoot down this field as pseudoscience. Someone makes a claim and seems genuine about what he saw, and someone else looks into it. Sometimes you discover that a species you thought was extinct is not, or animals that you thought existed only on other continents are also here. Why not Bigfoot? Why not lake monsters? Consistent claims are worth looking into. Here's where you come in, fellow legend trippers. Mainstream biologists and scientists rarely will chase those leads for fear of ridicule, which leaves the field of discovery wide open for people like us.

We will be discussing more cryptozoology, but I want to defend my "Monster Tripping" chapter title before we go further. Cryptozoologists would *not* study werewolves, vampires, or zombies, but dammit we will. Those legends are powerful, have roots in reality, and have invaded popular culture. They can't be ignored!

THUNDERBIRD

THE ALGONQUIAN-SPEAKING NATIONS of North America have in their legends a man-sized winged creature called a Pmola, or thunderbird. The thunderbird is described as a giant bird with glowing red eyes that swoops down and carries off animals and even people. The only warning the creature's victims receive is the deep *woosh* created by the Pmola's giant flapping wings.

The thunderbird is a powerful legend that has gone mainstream. The United States Air Force's exhibition team is called the Thunderbirds after this Native American legend, from the stories of Indians in the southwestern U.S., but we also know that the belief was strong in New England. In the Fruitlands Museum located in Harvard, Massachusetts, there is an exhibit that displays a Pennacook Indian artifact made of copper from the latter half of the sixteenth century. The shape is that of a winged creature with large eyes. The label on the piece reads "Thunderbird."

In many Native American cultures, the idea of a bird man exists and has been depicted in their art and lore.

MOTHMAN

THE DESCRIPTIONS AND LEGENDS of the thunderbird are eerily close to the descriptions of the Mothman—a creature infamous in paranormal circles that was reported by over 100 people in and around Point Pleasant, West Virginia, in 1966 and 1967.

The reason we know so much about the Mothman is because its sightings were so well-documented by cryptozoologist John Keel. The first documented sighting of the Mothman came at 10:30 p.m. on November 14, 1966, in Salem, West Virginia. Merle Partridge was watching television when the TV went out and made a "loud, whining noise." At that point his dog on the front porch began to howl toward the barn. Partridge grabbed his flashlight and shined the light in that direction. He claimed he saw two glowing red circles, or eyes—he said they looked like bicycle reflectors. The dog ran toward the creature, but Partridge got a cold chill and ran inside. His dog was never seen again.

The next night, a 1957 Chevrolet carrying two young couples, Mr. and Mrs. Roger Scarberry and Mr. and Mrs. Steve Mallette, were looking for friends in the same area. When they reached an old generator plant, Linda Scarberry gasped.

According to the Mothman Museum's Web site, Linda described what they saw: "It was shaped like a man, but bigger. Maybe six and a half or seven feet tall. And it had big wings folded against its back… But it was those eyes that got us. It had two big eyes like automobile reflectors. They were hypnotic. For a minute, we could only stare at it. I couldn't take my eyes off it."

The driver floored the gas pedal in an attempt to get back to the highway. They claimed the creature took off into the sky and after them. On Route 62 the automobile approached 100 miles per hour, but the creature was staying right with them—not even flapping its wings! When the car reached the city limits, the creature broke off and left the two couples, now en route to the sheriff's office to report what happened.

In the coming weeks and months, reports poured in from residents around Point Pleasant. As the accounts made the local and then national news, thousands flocked into the region hoping for their own sighting. If that's not legend tripping, I don't know what is. The witnesses were local, credible, and believable, and the legend of the Mothman grew.

As the Mothman legend spread, so too did the speculation as to what it was and where it came from. Some believed this creature to be the conjured result of black magic, others suggested that the nearby chemical plant had caused some kind of mutated creature to form, and another theory suggested the creature was the result of a Shawnee Indian curse.

For the next year, over 100 reports came in related to this half bird/half man creature with glowing red eyes. Then came December 1967—the Christmas season. On December 15, just after 5:00 p.m., as rush hour traffic moved across the Silver Bridge that spans the Ohio River between Point Pleasant and Kanauga, Ohio, something rumbled on the bridge, and then the structure collapsed beneath the weight of the cars, causing the death of 46 people.

The Mothman sightings in Point Pleasant ceased after December 15. Time offers the luxury of contemplation. Since the Mothman stopped lurking around Point Pleasant, many have come to speculate that the creature is some kind of harbinger of doom, and that it shows up only when something bad is going to happen. Who's to say there's any connection between the Mothman in Point Pleasant and the bridge collapsing? Why would this creature have insight into the future any more than we would?

Questions; It's what we come back to again and again because we can't sit the Mothman down for an interview (and believe me, I've tried—his agent won't return my calls). Kicking these theories around is a big part of legend tripping. It's the takeaway, the homework assignment you'll never finish no matter how much time you're given to work on it. *Them's the breaks.* If you want answers, you'll have to keep digging.

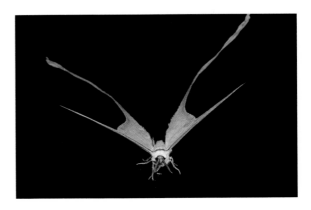

VAMPIRES

UNLESS YOU'RE COMPLETELY INSULATED from teen movies and popular culture, you know that vampires are a hot commodity right now. Thanks to the *Twilight* series, vampires are good looking and sexy, and they "sparkle." That's the face of vampires in the twenty-first century, but that will change, because the face of vampires always changes to remain relevant with the times.

Go back just 150 years or so, and you'll find vampires weren't quite so pretty. Vampires used to be the walking dead. They were victims of consumption, more commonly known by the modern name of tuberculosis. Tuberculosis is still a deadly disease in much of the world, though there are vaccines and treatments available today for those with access to modern medicine. It can afflict some people for decades, enabling them to survive to old age before succumbing, or it can run through a person's system in just a few weeks. Most commonly, consumption took its sweet time killing—torturing the victim's body and tormenting the minds and spirits of the victim's loved ones.

With death creeping through cities, towns, neighborhoods, and families, it's no surprise that many people looked for supernatural reasons that some families were spared while others were decimated by consumption. Is this punishment from God? Is it an attack by the Devil? Is there a vampire walking among us, draining the life from certain victims?

Today vampires are attractive, alluring, and full of life—a stark contrast to the original version of this monster.

When there is chaos, humans will find order. When medical science doesn't have an answer, folklore and legend will find one. Those ill with consumption often suffered violent coughing fits—especially in the night when they were lying on their backs and fluid had the chance to settle in the lungs. In the morning, blood might be found on the patient's chin, neck, or night-clothes—raising suspicion that this person was "feeding" in the night as opposed to coughing up blood. Near the end, the patient looks like the walking dead—skeleton-thin, frail, pale, almost a corpse. The only way to break the spell is to stop the undead vampire spreading the affliction. We'll get to that in a moment.

One New England vampire case that shocked the modern world happened in Exeter, Rhode Island, in 1892. Mercy Lena Brown was a farmer's daughter, one of three children. Consumption ravaged the Brown family.

During the 1800s, pulmonary tuberculosis was credited with one out of every four deaths. In the Brown family, that percentage was significantly higher. Consumption took its first victim within the family in December 1883, when Mercy's mother, Mary Brown, died of the disease. Seven months later, the Browns' eldest daughter, Mary Olive, died of consumption. The Browns' only son, Edwin, came down with consumption a few years after Mary Olive's death and was sent to live in the arid climate of Colorado to try and stop the disease. Late in 1891, Edwin returned home to Exeter because the disease was pro-gressing—essentially coming home to die.

Mercy's battle with consumption was consider-ably shorter than her brother's. Mercy had the "galloping" variety of consumption—her battle with the disease lasted only a few months. In January 1892, Mercy was laid to rest in Chestnut Hill Cemetery behind the Baptist church on Victory Highway. But that isn't where her story ends.

It's important to note when she died: January, the dead of winter in Rhode Island. Mercy would not have been put in the ground right away, she would have been placed in the stone keep on the property—the place where bodies were stored for the winter until the ground thawed and graves could be dug. As a safeguard (and to add significantly to the creepy factor), the keep had a bell hanging on the outside with a rope running to the inside. *Pourquoi,* you may ask? This is in case a body placed in the keep isn't dead; if a person wakes up, he can pull the rope to alert others and get some help.

NOTE

Here's a legend-tripping assignment for you: Try to find an historic account of a person being placed in a keep prematurely and tolling the bell to get help. Sweet dreams tonight, huh?

The keep where Mercy Brown's body was placed during
the winter to await burial in the spring.
Photo by Andrew Lake.

So with Mercy in the keep, the Brown family was down to two living members: George, the patriarch, and his son, Edwin, who was getting worse with consumption. Why would one family be so terribly cursed? Medicine had no answers for the Browns, but folklore did. The family was the victim of a vampire. They must identify the vampire and stop it—then there's a chance to save Edwin. Considering that the doctors had given up, George Brown was a man with nothing to lose.

On March 17, 1892, George entered the keep at Chestnut Hill Cemetery and had his daughter Mercy exhumed. The gathered witnesses were astounded to see that Mercy's body had shifted inside the keep. When they unwrapped her corpse, they saw few signs of decomposition… surely this must be the vampire! George Brown cut open the chest of his daughter's body and found liquid blood in her heart—a sign surely that she must be undead and still feeding on the living. Mercy's heart was removed and burned on a nearby rock, and the ashes of the heart were given to Edwin to eat to break the spell.

Two months later, Edwin also succumbed to consumption.

The Mercy Brown case continues to perplex us because it has never really left the public eye. Even back in 1892, the *Providence Journal* reported on the events surrounding Mercy Brown's exhumation. The gist of the article was "Look at what these bumpkins in southern Rhode Island are doing!" The point the newspaper missed is the power of legend and belief.

Mercy Brown's grave today.
Photo by Andrew Lake.

More than a century later, we can only speculate, but I'm willing to guess George Brown didn't expect the ritual to work for Edwin. He was a desperate man who lost his entire family to a disease. He was willing to try any remedy, no matter how ludicrous it may have sounded to others.

How was Mercy identified as the vampire? First, she died before the days of embalming, and she was kept in a virtual cooler for the months between her death and her being removed from the keep. We know that bodies can bloat, groan, jerk, and move themselves as decomposition works on a corpse. Muscles can grow tense, limbs can move, and blood can coagulate and then liquefy as bacteria eat away at flesh.

Many have claimed that the story of Mercy Brown played some inspiration to Bram Stoker, who penned the classic *Dracula*. Published in 1897, Stoker's vampire stepped away from the traditional folklore version of this monster to be a powerful and alluring creature. The vampire evolved and still does today.

Historically speaking, society has dealt with vampires in a myriad of ways. Driving a stake through the heart has less to do with spearing a once-vital organ with a piece of wood and more to do with literally nailing the corpse to the ground so it can't get up again. In some cases, the corpse was exhumed and then turned upside down so it couldn't leave its grave to attack the living.

The original point of driving a stake through a vampire's heart was to nail its body to the ground.

Archaeologist Matteo Borrini was on a dig on Lazzaretto Nuovo Island, uncovering a mass grave dating back to Venice's 1576 plague, when he uncovered the skeletal remains of a woman who had a brick placed neatly in her mouth after she died. We can only speculate that the brick was meant to keep this "vampire" from feeding on the living.

Vampires will continue to turn up, they will continue to be scapegoats when science fails to answer the mass's questions, and they will continue to evolve in popular culture as each new generation embraces what they believe a vampire should be.

This is one monster just about any legend tripper can find. If the historical vampire isn't your cup of blood, there are modern-day energy, or psychic, vampires and actual blood drinkers with a fetish who sharpen their teeth. Talk to all of them. Find out why they believe what they believe.

Vampires weren't just consumption victims, either. During the Black Plague that wiped out a third of Europe in the fourteenth and fifteenth centuries, some believed it wasn't disease sucking the life out the living, it was vampires. In March 2009, further evidence of historic vampires turned up in Venice, Italy, during an excavation.

Bran Castle in Romania is commonly called "Dracula's Castle" because of its ties to Vlad "The Impaler" Tepes.

GIANT WATER SERPENTS

AT THE BEGINNING OF THIS CHAPTER, I mentioned some of the creatures that were believed to be either extinct or myth, like the coelacanth. These cryptids (and the people who search for them) are scoffed at until an actual creature is discovered. The good news for legend trippers who want to contribute to the search for these kinds of creatures is that you can make valuable contributions to this field of research. You don't need to be a full-time scholar to get outside with your camera in hand and seek evidence that can shake up the world a little bit.

Sightings of giant water serpents have been reported for centuries. We mostly think of sea serpents, but there are also freshwater creatures such as the Loch Ness Monster or Champy in Lake Champlain, or even Tahoe Tessy in Lake Tahoe. Maybe those creatures are relics from the era of dinosaurs, maybe they're giant snakes, or maybe they're hoaxes.

The sea serpent has been making mainstream news for over a century. In August 1817, a 300-foot-long sea serpent visited Gloucester Harbor in Massachusetts so frequently that the creature was witnessed by hundreds of people—some of whom were perched on lawn chairs around the harbor, waiting to catch a glimpse.

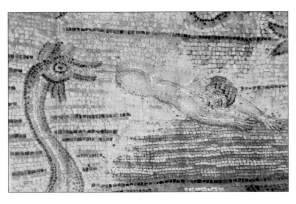

For centuries witnesses have reported giant sea creatures and serpents—monsters that have inspired us and brought fear to sailors.

Even today a video or photograph turns up and earns a spot on international news as people ponder what the camera reveals. In recent years, a water creature lurking in Madeira Beach canal in Florida made the news because it was caught on video tape on multiple occasions. You may have seen the clip featuring a large, dark head coming out of the water followed by a long body behind it. Is it a monster from hell? Probably not, but that doesn't mean we know what it is. Reviewing a video like this is legend trip enough for some people, but imagine taking the video! This story serves as a reminder to keep our cameras poised.

On the Hunt for a Troll

So there I was on Facebook.com when I posted a comment asking people in my network to send me a note about their favorite local legends. Soon I received an email from Kelly Mackinnon, telling me about cursed gates, a troll lurking in the woods of Dedham, Massachusetts, and even a little house said to be home to the troll. Cursed gates? A troll? She had my full attention. Mackinnon said:

I went down there when I was in high school so that was like ten years ago. And there's so many stories in Dedham, it's awesome. My mom used to live right down there so she knows all the stories and everything.

I grew up in Walpole, but my mom grew up in Dedham. She used to tell me stories and stuff about the houses down there and the supposed legends. She told me about "Hammer Road," and I heard the stories from a bunch of other people. They're like, "You gotta go down there, it's really creepy." So a bunch of us went down there one night. You drive down the street and it's just a really eerie feeling, and you see this whole stone wall, and you see three gates, and the story supposedly is the guy who used to live on that street had three children, killed his children, and then buried them under each one of the gates. So supposedly if you go down there, you shake the gates and you get into an accident, or you see strange things. Or if you jump the wall there's supposedly some troll thing that lived behind there and you see the house. It's just all these things.

So we jumped the wall one night and we're walking back in the woods and I heard what sounded like kids crying, screaming almost, you know? And there's nobody around because you're back there kind of far. And so I heard that and we're all like, "What was that?" You know? We figured it was just something from someone's house so we didn't think anything of it. We walked back further and we found this little tiny house. It looked like it was made not like what a normal house is made out of, but it was just constructed back there by something. We didn't go near it because we didn't know how sturdy it was, and you had to crawl over this bridge to get to it, so we didn't go near it. It was almost like a fort, like kids would go back there and build a fort, but it was more well constructed than that. It was definitely something out of the ordinary so you wouldn't expect it to be there.

It was so dark back there so you couldn't really see everything, but if it's still there, it's just awesome. So we heard these really strange noises. At the time we were 16, so we were really freaked out. So we kind of hung around for a minute and we heard some cackling in the woods and some screaming, so we booked it out of there. But the whole time we would swear that we heard someone walking behind us and kind of like footsteps behind us. It was just so creepy we jumped the wall and got out of there. (laughs) You go down there and it's just so cool. I'd love to go back there.

It's odd to see these normal-sized gates and then this one smaller opening gate thing. So we were like, "Hmmm, maybe this *is* true." So that's one of the reasons we went down there.

Kelly hadn't been to the troll gate in about 12 years, but she got her wish to go back sooner than she expected. The next morning she agreed to accompany and guide me on a legend trip to the road where "troll gate" could be found, and show me around. On the ride to Dedham, she confessed that she went there the night before around midnight with one of her friends so she could remember where it was. She said she saw a carful of kids snooping around the gates and stone walls, which means the legend must still be alive and well in Dedham.

The name of the road is actually Westfield Street; it runs through an upscale neighborhood with some large houses. During our drive up the road, the weather was overcast with a hint of rain—late March in Massachusetts—a perfect addition to the creepy factor. As we rounded a bend, I saw a tall, imposing stone wall a few feet from the edge of the road. The hilly terrain and long wall make it look almost like a fortress. The tall barrier implies maybe there's something hidden in the woods just beyond.

Further up the road, we see the first gate. There's a visual dichotomy here: In the front the gate is old, rusty, and right out of a horror movie. Directly behind that is a new-looking chain link fence with a warning sign: M.I.T. Property No Trespassing Police Take Notice. I soon learn that, yes, it's *that* M.I.T.—the Massachusetts Institute of Technology.

The imposing stone wall that runs along the side of Westfield Street that contains a legendary gate.

After passing the first gate, we soon see the second—the alleged "troll gate." Even at first glance I can see it's smaller than the other. Not tiny, but also not convenient. I would have to duck to walk through, whereas the first gate I could have strolled right under if it were open.

The car reaches the third gate in the wall, which looks similar to the first. After passing all three gates, the wall ends for a driveway and large house on a hillside. Kelly says that's the house where the man supposedly lived who killed his three children and buried one under each gate.

A little further up the road we see another end to the wall and a path—but this path has no "no trespassing" signs. We turn around at the end of the cul-de-sac and park across from the path. The woods are hilly and quiet once we go just a few yards down the path. It's here that Kelly tells me her story again.

There is no substitute for hearing a first-hand account in the vicinity of the actual event. This is legend tripping gold. I can see the sparkle and wonder as she retells her tale, which took place just behind where we are standing.

The middle/smaller gate that some locals have dubbed "troll gate."

Let's sum up:

► The gates are there, and behind them lay acres of forest.

► The house where the man who allegedly murdered his three children is there.

► The troll house? Well, we don't know.

No one believes the house was built by or for a troll, but combine the structure with the little gate, the other paranormal tales, and the eyewitness account of screams in the night, and you have a great legend.

ANALYZING MONSTER EVIDENCE

WITH SO MANY PEOPLE LEGEND tripping today and so many cell phone cameras, more visual evidence than ever before is coming forward. These are exciting times for legend tripping, to be sure. But the waters can quickly get murky. When presented with evidence such as a photograph, it's our duty to pick it apart as best we can. If we can explain it away, we take the evidence off the table. If we can't...well now, that's why we're here, isn't it?

TIP

If you're in the field and see something unexplained—grab your camera! Please, oh please, keep clicking photos until your finger is sore. And if the unexplained *thing* moves/runs/vanishes, keep clicking.

Photos taken just before, during, and after a sighting are very helpful in giving us perspective of time, distance, and size. Later, once you've calmed down, you can go back where you were standing and put a person into the shot where the phenomenon was spotted. You might be surprised to learn that the giant mountain cat wasn't a giant at all. When a human is standing in the same place, photo comparison may show the "giant" cat would not have come up much higher than an adult's shins.

BIGFOOT

BIGFOOT GOES BY MANY NAMES but few descriptions. In Ohio he's called the Grassman of Ohio, in some cultures he's Sasquatch, and I know of one western Massachusetts town that dubbed their version "The Monster of Coca-Cola Ledge" (so-called because he's been spotted on a high ledge that boasted a painted Coca-Cola logo for many years). This creature—or at the very least the idea of this creature—has been around for centuries.

Some Bigfoot researchers take a very pragmatic approach to their work. They figure it's just an uncategorized North American ape that we haven't been able to pin down yet. Others, such as author Nick Redfern, will tell you, "I think he's more paranormal than that." There's another theory that this creature is an alien, and the reason we can't find its home or a corpse is because it goes back to its spaceship or to its dimension. It's legend tripping, folks. You have to listen to the stories, do your research, and find evidence to support what you believe. Get to it!

Online Resources for Bigfoot Research:

The Bigfoot Field Researchers Organization: www.bfro.net

Alliance of Independent Bigfoot Researchers: www.bigfootresearch.com

The American Bigfoot Society: www.americanbigfootsociety.com

Though he goes by many names, people know what you mean when you say "Bigfoot."

There are many other sites—some specific to regions or states. Each of these sites allows you to review evidence, read first-hand accounts, and peruse the research.

STUMBLING INTO BIGFOOT

ON JULY 25, 2009, Maine-based paranormal investigator Jason Lorefice was spending the day exploring the Hockomock Swamp—specifically, the paranormal legends of the "Bridgewater Triangle," a roughly 200-square-mile area of southeastern Massachusetts that falls between the towns of Freetown, Rehoboth, and Abington. Lorefice was riding his bicycle down a road that cuts through part of the Hockomock Swamp when he noticed a set of oversized footprints in the mud just off to the side of the street leading into the cornfield adjacent to the road. He stopped to get a closer look. Lorefice said, "As I examined the prints closer, I noticed that a trail of them looked as if someone or something had crossed the road and into the cornfield, where it made its way toward the swamp. I did, in fact, see some of the crops pushed aside as if something large had passed through it."

The large footprint discovered by Jason Lorefice in Bridgewater, Massachusetts.
Photo courtesy of Jason Lorefice.

Stumbling across evidence like this is every legend tripper's dream. There are so many things you want to do simultaneously, including track the creature if you can, preserve the evidence, or call in some experts. Lorefice continued: "Due to the fact that it was late in the afternoon, I was faced with two options: either pursue the tracks into the thick dense brush and try to track it—or race back into town and buy some plaster of Paris at Home Depot and make a mold of one of the tracks. When I returned to the site with plaster, I also measured the tracks and found some inconsistencies in the stride pattern. The first five tracks had a stride length of approximately 87 inches from heel to toe. The next four after that measured approximately 78 to 79 inches. The length of the feet was about 18 long by 7 inches (in the widest part of the foot). My guess was, if it had been a person's foot, they would have to be at least 8 1/2 feet tall."

Jason Lorefice poses with his footprint cast.
Photo courtesy of Jason Lorefice.

HOW TO MAKE A MOLD OF A FOOTPRINT IN THE DIRT OR MUD.

Okay, legend trippers, this is something you might want to practice at home before heading out into the field.

If you find a footprint, you'll want to make a plaster mold. Buy some plaster of Paris at just about any hardware or craft store. Mix two cups of the powder with one and a half cups of water in a bucket.

Stir the mixture until it's smooth and the air bubbles are out. Gently pour the mixture into the footprint you're trying to preserve. You may want to build a frame of cardboard around the footprint so you can fill the box and print.

Now wait. The longer you can leave the plaster to dry, the better. Weather and your travel plans may not allow for a full 12 hours, but give it at least an hour. If you pour a thick mold, expect it to take more drying time.

Jason Lorefice captured his footprint and had an amazing story to tell. Even today he can't promise he's not the victim of a hoax. But if he is a victim, no one has come forward yet, laughing. If someone placed fake footprints deliberately, it's possible they never would have been found. In that stretch of road, very few people walk by. I know because I went to check it out.

The area where the print was taken is a Bigfoot hotspot. Large, hairy creatures have been reported in the area for many years. Lorefice's footprint just adds to the legend.

TIP

Bring your audio recorder! Much of the evidence collected by Bigfoot researchers is audio. If you're camping near where a sighting occurred or hiking through the wilderness in Sasquatch territory, you want your audio recorder at the ready in case you hear a howl or sound that isn't familiar.

If you hear something, be quiet! Hold still, and record for as long as you hear the noise. When it's done, tag the recording with your voice. Something like: "It's Saturday, March 27, 2010, at 3:17 p.m., we're about one mile down the trail leading east from where we parked our car. The sound seemed to be coming from the north of us." If you have a portable GPS device, now is the perfect time to take a reading and tag the specific location in your recording and notes (recordings, sadly, can sometimes be deleted by accident). Also, take some pictures of where you are in case you want to go back later.

A video camera can accomplish all of this on video and save a step.

As a last step, you need to review the audio. Don't worry, I'm not an animal call expert, either. But that doesn't mean you can't do some sleuthing on your own first to rule out some known animal.

STEP 1. Identify what animals are normally found in the area where you captured the audio.

STEP 2. Narrow your search of animals based on your best guess. For example, if you're certain it's not a bird, you eliminate that category. However, don't be so sure until you've really developed an ear for animal sounds. If you have a hunch, you can access an amazing online resource: The Cornell Lab of Ornithology Macaulay Library at www.macaulaylibrary.org. The site has thousands of animal sounds and photographs available free. You can hear examples of various calls to see if you might have a match to something known.

STEP 3. If you are out of guesses, then it's time to reach out to the pros. If you seek a local wildlife expert, you're much more likely to get help from someone you don't know if you show the steps you've taken already. Consider wildlife conservation groups or state park rangers for a referral to someone who might be able to identify an animal sound. Begin with the organizations closest to where you made your recording. If you can get a park ranger perplexed, you're on to something good. See it through!

ZOMBIES

I'M A SUCKER FOR ZOMBIE MOVIES.
Always have been. If the undead rise to walk the earth and want to eat our brains or turn us into other zombies, I'm there. The zombie genre has been alive and well in cinema for almost as long as there has been cinema. And like most great monster tales, there's a basis in folklore.

There's a passage in the Bible that references dead bodies rising up. Matthew 27:50–53 says, "And when Jesus had cried out again in a loud voice, he gave up his spirit. At that moment the curtain of the temple was torn in two from top to bottom. The earth shook and the rocks split. The tombs broke open and the bodies of many holy people who had died were raised to life. They came out of the tombs, and after Jesus' resurrection they went into the holy city and appeared to many people."

Raising the dead as a religious theme isn't exclusive to Christianity. In some cases these stories are metaphorical—meaning the body isn't raised from the dead, just the soul or spirit—but in other cases it is literal, as when Jesus raised Lazarus from the dead.

Reanimating a corpse is a theme that speaks to something very primal and very dark. It's why the Frankenstein story works so well and why Stephen King's *Pet Sematary* scares us. Raising the dead is the single biggest offense to nature. If we could do it, God knows what might come back.

Braaains...they want to eat your braaaains.

Nowhere is the notion of a zombie more prevalent than in voodoo cultures, especially Haiti. Folk magic combines with folklore to produce tangible evidence. This concept has been well documented by Wade Davis, a researcher who went to Haiti to study the process of making zombies and presented his findings in the popular book (later made into a movie of the same name) *The Serpent and the Rainbow*. Davis concluded that the zombie-making process involves making a magic powder that includes a toxin, temporarily rendering its victim paralyzed to the point of appearing deceased. The body is then buried, the witch doctor quickly digs up the victim, and once the victim regains consciousness, the witch doctor convinces him he is a zombie and is now owned by the witch doctor. If the victim believes this to be true…guess what? It is.

With the exception of the myriad of zombie movies, actual accounts don't dot the landscape much outside of the Caribbean voodoo influence.

That doesn't mean people can't relocate and bring their folk magic, rituals, and belief with them. The world is smaller than ever, and those alleged creatures are free to show up outside of their home territories.

A good legend tripper is always listening for these types of tales and checking them out. By knowing the roots of the legend, we can quickly figure out how a zombie might appear in, say, Texas. If we dig in, do we find people of Haitian origin or close acquaintances of people of Haitian origin near the story? Or do we have something entirely new?

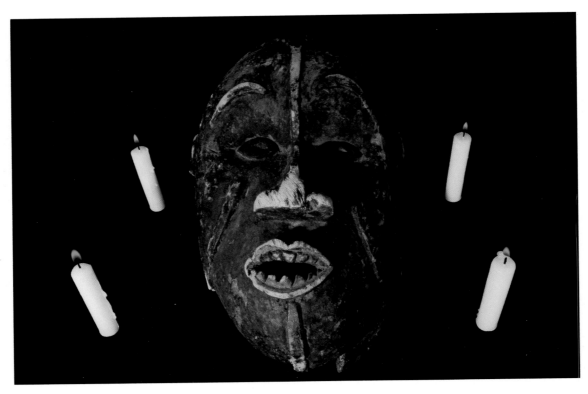

CHUPACABRA

LITERALLY "GOAT SUCKER," the Chupacabra is a cryptid from Latino lore—specifically Puerto Rico. It spread to other Caribbean countries, parts of South America, Central America, and the southern United States. In recent years, the creature has also been reported in Maine and even in Russia. Considering the legend goes back only to roughly 1995, this is of high intrigue to legend trippers—we should be able to follow the stories with great accuracy.

The creature is described as monkey-like, standing four to five feet tall, with oval red eyes that glow in some reports, gray skin, a long snake-like tongue, fangs, spiny quills along its back, and sometimes wings. It's a monster, though, by all descriptions and not just because of the way it looks. The name "Chupacabra" was coined by Puerto Rican comedian and broadcast host Silverio Pérez. "Goat sucker" stuck because the creature is said to descend on livestock, leaving multiple puncture wounds in the chest and draining the helpless animals of blood, then leaving their corpses (sometimes by the dozens) for farmers to find the next morning.

By the end of 1995, Chupacabras were blamed for over 1,000 mysterious animal deaths involving blood loss through one or more puncture wounds. In 1996, reports turned up in Miami, Florida, southern Texas, and Juarez, Mexico. The legend was spreading and leaving dead farm animals in its wake.

In August 2008, some video from a police squad car shot near Cuero, Texas, shows a canine-looking creature trotting up a road in front of the police car. When the creature turns its head, a long snout is revealed. Chupacabra purists will claim the animal in this video doesn't come close to matching the right description, but the word "Chupacabra" was the implication many media outlets reached—another example of people wanting to label everything, even if that label is paranormal.

The search for monsters and cryptids is a quest humans have been on since man could hunt and ask questions. In some respects, it is the first in a line of much bigger questions, because you can't explore the paranormal and the universe before you know what creatures dwell in your own back yard.

These dragons, beasts, monsters, and demonic creatures hold us under their spell. The reason these subjects work so well in books and movies is that we understand on a very deep level what they are; we understand because generations of our ancestors talked about these creatures and the powers they may or may not possess.

If you're ready, grab your gear, your bug repellent, and meet me outdoors. We're on the trail of legendary monsters!

UFO

TRIPPING

"Space, the final frontier.
These are the voyages of the starship Enterprise.
Her five-year mission: to explore strange new worlds,
to seek out new life and new civilizations,
to boldly go where no man has gone before."

—Captain James T. Kirk

THE STUDY OF UFOS, OR UFOLOGY, began July 8, 1947, in Roswell, New Mexico, when an alleged UFO crash near a U.S. military base made front-page news and sparked a debate that continues to this day. Many UFO purists don't like the idea of discussing this topic as part of legend or folklore, but the reality is that one person's ghost is another person's alien. The reason we hear about famous sightings or abductions is because a story spread like pollen in a spring breeze and drew people in to find out more.

Long before 1947, humans watched the stars with wonder. Plenty of accounts in religious texts and history books mention UFOs. We have to remember that UFO stands for Unidentified Flying Object. Though the definition is self-explanatory, it bears repeating: It's flying, and you can't identify it. That doesn't mean what you're seeing isn't something natural or made by humans. But the possibility also exists that what you're seeing is from another galaxy or dimension—if you don't accept this possibility, then legend tripping isn't for you.

There are "billions and billions of stars," as the late, great astronomer Carl Sagan used to say. That's billions and billions of opportunities for planets to have developed near enough to a star so temperatures aren't too hot or too cold. Add in some water, and *bam*—you have billions of opportunities to spawn life as *we* know it. That doesn't mean there aren't life forms that evolved in completely different environments.

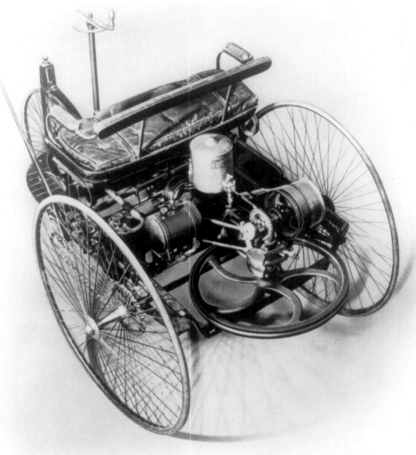

The Benz three-wheeler, made in 1885, which was the first practical automobile using an internal combustion engine. Courtesy of the Library of Congress.

The current estimate is that the universe is 13.75 billion years and 27 minutes old. Considering there are galaxies that formed millions of years before our own and millions of years after ours, it's ludicrous to think there can't be civilizations out there that are significantly more advanced than our own. Look at how far technology has come in under one hundred years. We have gone from the internal combustion engine to air travel to space travel.

Imagine where we'll be in just a thousand years (an eye blink of time in terms of the age of the universe) if we don't blow ourselves up first. To think this vast universe exists solely for the few of us on this insignificant blue ball is a wholly egocentric view with no base in logic.

I mentioned my own childhood UFO sighting in Chapter 1, "Introduction." In this chapter, we'll hear from others and learn how to approach and document those legends.

Less than 100 years later, man landed on the moon.

UFOs in Religious Texts

MANY UFOLOGISTS BELIEVE the Bible also holds tales of UFO encounters. In 2 Kings 2:11, the Bible reads: "As they [Elijah and Elisha] were going along and talking, behold, there appeared a chariot of fire and horses of fire which separated the two of them. And Elijah went up by a whirlwind to heaven."

Could the Bible be describing a vehicle descending with rockets blazing and some kind of tractor beam bringing Elijah up to a ship? Thousands of years ago the people of Earth would have had no way to comprehend a flying machine of any kind. They would do their best to reconcile what they saw with what they knew. It's worth noting the Bible uses the terms "chariot" and "horses"—both were commonly understood modes of transportation from one place to another, and they could move at relatively high speed. If people—whose knowledge of transportation was boats, chariots, and beasts of burden—saw something new in the sky, it would make sense that they would compare it to another mode of transportation that they *did* understand.

Also in the Bible, Isaiah 66:15 reads: "For behold, the LORD will come in fire; And His chariots like the whirlwind, To render His anger with fury, And His rebuke with flames of fire."

The Bible makes several references to anomalies in the sky that could be interpreted as UFOs.

Again the imagery of chariots, fire, and whirlwinds comes into play. It's not a reach to see it's possible they view beings coming down from the heavens as having great power. And should they unleash their fury on humans, there's little we could do.

In Erich von Daniken's best-selling book, *Chariot of the Gods?*, he speculates that perhaps we've been visited by intelligent beings from other worlds for millennia, and maybe humans have since turned these regular beings into gods.

Signs are everywhere. How we interpret these signs is the key.

UFOs over North America

THE FIRST DOCUMENTED UFO sighting in North America took place in the vicinity of Boston, Massachusetts, in 1638 and was chronicled by then-Governor John Winthrop. Winthrop wrote:

"In this year one James Everell, a sober, discreet man, and two others, saw a great light in the night at Muddy River. When it stood still, it flamed up, and was about three yards square; when it ran, it was contracted into the figure of a swine: it ran as swift as an arrow towards Charlton, and so up and down about two or three hours. They were come down in their lighter about a mile, and, when it was over, they found themselves carried quite back against the tide to the place they came from. Divers[e] other credible persons saw the same light, after, about the same place."

James Everell was a pig farmer. The "swine" was a familiar shape to him, his brain forced him to matrix this unidentified object into something he could understand. What Gov. Winthrop wrote is all that was written about this encounter. We could all learn something about the governor's reporting style: objective facts, he comments on the character of the witness, and he makes no speculation as to what this thing could have been.

Gov. John Winthrop of Massachusetts (1588–1649).
Courtesy of the Library of Congress.

CLOSE ENCOUNTERS

Thanks to Steven Spielberg's 1977 hit movie, many of us know what "close encounters of the third kind" means—contact with an alien. But there are actually seven close encounter categories (though not every group agrees on using all seven):

FIRST: A UFO sighting.

SECOND: Seeing a UFO and feeling some kind of physical effect—this could be things such as feeling heat from the craft as it passes by, radio interference as you see it, startled animals or livestock, or damage to the ground from a landing.

THIRD: Seeing a being of some kind in association with a UFO. This could mean seeing the being in a window or portal on the craft or seeing one on the ground near a landing site.

FOURTH: When a human is abducted by the UFO or beings inside and physical contact is made.

FIFTH: Kind of like a voluntary joint human-alien summit. When the humans and the aliens willingly meet of their own accord.

SIXTH: A UFO incident that causes injury or death to the human. Many consider this category to be redundant with the fourth kind.

SEVENTH: The Black Vault Encyclopedia Project proposed this category to include entity contact that results in human-alien hybridization. That's right, cross-breeding.

CLOSE ENCOUNTER OF THE FIRST KIND
HOW FOUR MINUTES CAN ATTACH ITSELF
TO A PERSON FOR A LIFETIME

WE'RE ALL A PRODUCT of our upbringing and environment. We all have baggage we carry with us everywhere—it's our exposure to religion, our level of education, our income, the friends we have, our occupation, our chemical dependencies, and our psychological makeup. How we deal with any person or event depends on what's in our baggage.

Most of the time, our personal development is slow and steady, but all of us have experienced events so big they become part of us and change us forever. These big events are usually brief and are never planned. A paranormal encounter is one of those life-altering events.

Legend tripping is about networking with fellow enthusiasts and talking to as many people as you can about these amazing subjects—it's a big part of the adventure. I called my buddy Matt Moniz (you've seen his mug throughout this book and in the DVD with this book) and said, "Hey, I want to interview someone who has taken some compelling UFO photos."

"You know Joe Ferriere in Woonsocket [Rhode Island]?" Matt asked.

No, I didn't.

"He's got this old record store with all kinds of weird collectibles," Matt said. "You should go see him."

Matt giving me a UFO sighting tip—nothing beats a great network of legend-tripping friends.

I did a little Googling and found the store: Joe's Moldy Oldies in Woonsocket, Rhode Island. I called the store, and Joe answered. He wasn't interested in talking about an event that took place over 40 years ago, but he told me he wrote everything up in a magazine he published back then called *Probe*. He said he'd make sure a copy was in his store the following day for me. I figured in person I'd have a better chance at getting him to open up.

The following day I leave the house armed with my backpack containing my camera, audio recorder, and video recorder…because you never know.

It's rainy. I mean a deluge, the worst rain on record for this region ever. The going is slow, but steady. I roll up to his store on a side street of Woonsocket. The building looks forgotten—an old shop on the first floor, apartments on the two floors above. I would have passed by if I wasn't looking for this place.

I step out into the street, which looks almost like a river as a quarter inch of water races down to the intersection below. The window to Joe's Moldy Oldies is covered with signs and memorabilia, but mostly dirt. It's difficult to see inside. It looks dark, but there's an "open" sign. I jog to the door because of the rain. The doorframe is swollen from the moisture, but a push from my shoulder causes it to give way.

The store was aptly named. Magazines, books, DVDs, VHS tapes, sports memorabilia, and occult and UFO curiosities were everywhere. There were so many colors and covers screaming for my attention that it became a kind of tchotchke camouflage—I see all of it and none of it at the same time. Standing in the middle like a statue, with one foot perched on a chair and watching the small television in the corner, was Joe. His hair was jet black, and his pencil-thin mustache didn't waver. His head turned to notice me before turning back to the TV.

"Hi Joe, I'm Jeff," I say.

"That's what I figured," he replies. Not friendly, not unfriendly either.

"You mind if I look around first?"

"Go right ahead," he says. And he's back to his television watching. I step carefully because Joe's moldy oldies are *everywhere*—at my feet, at eye level, and on shelves above. I see books authored by friends of mine, and I see a magazine for sale that I wrote an article for. I see other magazines for sale that I used to get for free and have since thrown out figuring no one would want them, let alone pay for them.

Joe Ferriere holding the September 1968 issue of his *Probe* magazine.

I compliment Joe on his store. And I mean it. I could easily spend a day digging in here. The best legend-tripping interviews take place as soon as possible after an encounter, but there's something about speaking with someone decades later that also has magic. When he stands by what he's been saying, when he has the benefit of all of those years, the sleepless nights, the postulating, only then does he have some insight on what it may mean (at least to him).

I ask Joe about his sighting and he starts to talk. The barrier that was there on the phone is gone now. I quickly reach for my audio recorder. I ask Joe if I can record our conversation. He says I can.

JOE FERRIERE

As I recall I was rather calm about the whole thing. There wasn't a feeling of fright or anything, it just felt perfectly normal for this to be here and for me to be watching this [he laughs].

This was one of many, many sightings that took place in the whole East Woonsocket area in 1966 and '67. In fact, there were busloads of people who would come down from Boston and points north to sky watch. That's how many UFOs were being seen.

There was a mindset of that time: All things are possible, the impossible just takes a little bit longer. As you get older, at least I got to be a little more crotchety, a little more difficult to convince. But that was a magical period of time—that was not my only sighting, by the way.

Ferriere goes on to explain another daylight sighting he had a few years earlier where he saw three craft in the sky over Rhode Island. Because he was already exploring the subject and publishing a magazine called *Probe*, when something UFO-related happens in the area, people call Joe.

So there Ferriere was in Cumberland, Rhode Island, around 6:30 p.m. on July 3, 1967. For three days prior, he had been fielding three or four phone calls per day about a large cylindrical UFO in the area of the Pawtucket Reservoir, so he had to look for himself. With camera in hand, he pulled in to an area west of Diamond Hill Road. He walked along the trail beneath the power lines. According to his written account in *Probe* magazine, Ferriere found a clearing about 700 to 800 feet from the road and began searching for physical evidence of something out of the ordinary. He admits he didn't know what he was looking for and that he could have walked right over something and not known it. Forty-five minutes in, he was about to call off his search when he turned northwest and froze in his tracks.

He saw a large, cigar-shaped craft moving silently toward his position. He estimates the craft was 75 to 100 feet in length and flying about 150 to 200 feet above the ground (given that the tallest trees in the area were about 60 feet tall). He described the object as being a drab gray in color, and it had four circle-shaped lighter spots running along the length of the craft. He also observed a "piston-like apparatus" that slowly moved in and out of one end of the craft. The third distinguishing feature was a trap door-like form on the bottom.

Ferriere got to work taking pictures with his camera, clicking a picture, advancing the film, then sometimes running (and almost falling) to another position to take more photos. While he was watching this silent craft, the hatch opened, and he saw a shiny object launched from inside at a high rate of speed—faster than any jet plane by his estimate. Ferriere clicked more photos of the cigar until it accelerated and passed out of sight over the hill. Then he saw a disc-shaped object that had been ejected from the main craft hovering above the tree line. He also captured a photo of that craft before it quickly accelerated in the same direction of the larger ship.

Ferriere estimates the entire sighting lasted about four minutes. Even when he wrote up his experiences for his magazine, Ferriere refused to speculate as to what (or more accurately *where*) he believed this craft to be from.

Today I ask him for his perspective.

JOE FERRIERE

Now in my later years, I'm seriously considering this may have been an early experimentation with a stealth balloon. I think a lot of the evidence points in that direction. You really have to kind of stretch for alternative explanations.

Now we know a lot more than we did then about our own aeronautical advances, and more and more it seems to me that a large preponderance of reports can be attributed to experimental craft of one sort or another, including the possibility in some cases of holographic projection, so much so as to almost obliterate the possibility of ET visitations as far as I'm concerned. I don't rule it out. One would have to be incredibly naïve to rule out the possibility. I think you've got to look at all reasonable explanations and possibilities before you go that route.

Ferriere's eyes hardly move away from the TV in the corner as he tells his story and gives his opinion. I've seen the photos he's taken. He was kind enough to allow me to reprint the page from his magazine in this book. After reminding myself this was 1967, I have formed my own opinions. I invite you to do the same.

Decades later, people like me still seek out people like Joe Ferriere. As one last step in this legend trip, I make the journey to the power lines near Diamond Hill Road in Cumberland. With still and video cameras in hand, I park my car in the small parking lot of James H. Lynch Jr. Memorial Park on the side of the road and step out. I hike up the trail that follows the power line towers and start clicking pictures. I don't expect to see anything in the sky, but then again, neither did Joe on that fateful day.

A scan of *Probe* magazine featuring the photos Ferriere took in 1967.
Courtesy of Joe Ferriere.

©1968 Joseph L. Ferriere   7

Another photo from the *Probe* magazine featuring Ferriere's photos.
Courtesy of Joe Ferriere.

Joe Ferriere's sighting area today.

A Close Encounter of the Fourth Kind

THE MOST FRIGHTENING EXPERIENCE I can think of is being abducted against your will by anyone. When you believe the abductor to be not of this Earth, that fear is compounded significantly. I first met Audrey Hewins and her twin sister Debbie Hewins at a conference in Massachusetts in 2008. The pair started an organization called Starborn Support (www.starbornsupport.com)—an alien abduction support group for people who believe they have gone through this experience.

Audrey claims she's been experiencing abductions for as long as she can remember. "I remember having contacts from being in the crib," she said. "They've been around me and my sister our entire lives. The bald men, we called them. I even had journal entries of them." For her, the occurrence happens as frequently as every month or two.

Hewins also believes she's being followed by the factions of the United States government and has produced many photographs of black helicopters to support her claim. She believes her phones have been tapped and that larger forces are always monitoring her activities.

An interesting side note relating to this author's personal experience: I had Audrey and her sister as call-in guests on my talk show, *30 Odd Minutes*. I should say I *tried* to have them on, but our phone connection failed miserably during the live show. Sure, those things do happen, but it had never happened before or since. *Hmmm.* Then, the first time I tried to interview Audrey over the phone about her experiences for this book, we spoke for 23 minutes and 27 seconds. I know because I recorded our conversation (with her full knowledge and permission). Nothing came out on my recorder. Just some occasional static. I've used this phone recording system at least 100 times before with no failure (and no failure since). *Hmmm.* I'm not a conspiracy-prone person, but even I had to scratch my head here.

I did manage to get my interview with Audrey and record it on a second attempt a few weeks later—third time was the charm, I guess. Here's another interview tip. If your recording equipment fails and you need to interview the same person about the same subject again, try to let as much time as possible pass. If you conduct the interview the next day, the answers will come out sounding rehearsed, and corners will be cut on details. The first interview is always the best.

AUDREY HEWINS

The age that I most remember things happening is probably between seven and nine. There were times that I remember when I was younger, but you know the times that we actually became aware that something was happening I was about seven years old. What would happen was I'd get this really strange feeling. There was a kind of presence in the room that let you know something was going to happen. We thought if we hid under the covers nothing would happen to us, so we'd do that, but we noticed that our bodies would start to… I don't know what the word is… I guess kind of twitch, and it would be to a point when we couldn't move any of our limbs anymore. And we'd hear a steady humming sound like a generator or a bunch of bees getting closer and then farther away. At this point we could only move our eyes and then we'd notice that there was movement underneath our door. We'd see the door open, the light, and two figures would come in. One was taller than the other one so we'd call one of them the tall bald man and then the short bald man.

I was on the bottom bunk and my twin sister would be on the top bunk during the earlier experiences. We just wouldn't be able to move and then we'd kind of wake up a little while later. Our bodies kind of felt weird. Sometimes we'd have bloody noses. We'd be in different beds, in the wrong beds, upside down, different clothes on, I mean stuff like that would happen when we came to.

A lot of times before they came into our room they would make us feel almost comfortable by making us think it was our parents coming in. I guess it's kind of like screen memories that they do. They do that a lot.

The abductees think it's a totally different situation when it's not. And it's strange because once you realize that it is not real, that it is something that they're doing, then it's almost as if you can see them for their true selves.

Audrey Hewins.

Do you think these visitors had malicious intent?

I think we've got two different sides here. I know I've had some very unpleasant experiences, but I've also had some good experiences with a different race [of ET]. So I think there's a light and a dark side. It's a real thing. And there's also different energies that they put out. Now when I'm going to have a malevolent experience I know it because the feeling is different that I get before they come. It's absolute fear, really high anxiety. And then when they come and they actually enter the room the energies that you get in your physical body, it's incredible, I can't even explain it, but it's definitely a negative feeling.

How much notice do you get before an abduction?

If they're going to come on a certain night, I'll know maybe eight to twelve hours ahead of time just by the way I feel. Not all the time, though. Sometimes they sneak up. It depends on which ones are coming. When the better ones—the ones I feel are benevolent—you almost anticipate it, you know. It's exciting because they're just so different than the other ones that are scary [she laughs]. It's two different worlds when it comes to the energies.

When you feel like an abduction is coming, have you ever tried to set up a video camera on yourself while you're sleeping or anything like that?

I've tried to have my recorders going. The thing is with that, the electrical stuff, it all goes out. I know there's some kind of equipment I think that a certain group is using, I'm not sure who it is, but when I was interviewed by a member of MUFON they had asked if we wanted to have that stuff set up, but when I asked him who was doing it he really didn't know, so I really didn't want that. I don't want that kind of publicity. I'd like to do it myself, but things like the clock radio short out. Things just don't work anymore when they come.

What happened during one of your more memorable abductions?

This is kind of a scary experience, but one where I remember very vividly in every detail. It was back in November of 2006. I knew they were going to come. I had that feeling all day. So I was lying in my bed and I began to have the feelings, and my body started to twitch, and I said, "Here we go…" Then I started to hear the buzzing sound. I ended up waking through the process—I assume I'm usually sleeping at this time when they're in the room surrounding my bed and getting ready to take me. What happened was I woke up and I remember everything… it seems to be the same ones [entities] that have come for me ever since I was little. At least the tall one is always the same.

So he was standing at the end of my bed and I looked to each side of my bed and there were two of the smaller ones standing to each side. So there were five in my room. I panicked, and I grabbed one that was up near my right arm near the head of my bed. I grabbed him by his throat and when I grabbed him I could hear—it wasn't like they were *talking but it was a telepathy thing—but I heard them say, "Watch out for the mother," is what I hear and I let go. I didn't understand what that meant at all. I was somehow able to fight the paralysis this time and this was the last time that they used this kind of treatment on me—I'll fill you in with that detail afterward. But anyway, I got to my feet and was able to make it to my bedroom door as they were fighting me, and when I opened the bedroom door there were two other ones standing outside the door so I couldn't make it out of the room. And that's when they used—I don't know what it was they used on me but I guess it's a more powerful thing to paralyze me. I've talked to several abductees who said when they fight it they get the same treatment. If you move a muscle it feels like your muscle is on fire, it just burns. So you're completely incapacitated. And that's all I remember.*

I woke up—they had kind of just thrown me in the bed. Usually they tuck you in, they're pretty good about it—but they weren't happy that night [she laughs]. I guess they just realized I know what happens, there's no hiding it tonight.

The next time they came, which was maybe a month later, that same one that I had grabbed remembered me and he actually hit me in the head. He was in the same position, and then they used that burning stuff on me and we did it all over again. Whatever they do, wherever they take me, I don't know.

Audrey says she has flashes of consciousness from being on board the ship. She's even recognized people on Earth from being on the ship. She said there was an instant connection with those people, and she was grateful to be able to talk about the abduction with someone else. Debbie Hewins echoed many similar sentiments and experiences when I interviewed her. Both sisters believe they will be dealing with these abductions for the rest of their lives.

I hope one day Audrey is able to set up cameras and equipment on a day she feels something is coming. I'd love to be a legend-tripping fly on the wall when that happens.

KNOW YOUR LIMITATIONS

When studying UFOs, know your limitations. That means don't jump to conclusions if you aren't well versed in astronomy. Meteorites can light up a night sky, create sonic booms, and even bounce off the atmosphere, giving the appearance of something mechanical and deliberate. Also, know your body's limitations. Stare at anything long enough, and your mind will play tricks.

Here's a test: Go out on a starry night and stare directly at a single star or planet. Focus intently. The star *will* disappear. No, your mind didn't just obliterate Polaris like some *Star Wars*-ian Death Star; your eyes simply don't focus well in low light. Know your limitations so you can separate natural phenomena from artificial.

UNIDENTIFIED SUBMERSIBLE OBJECTS—USOs

YOU'VE HEARD ABOUT UNIDENTIFIED Flying Objects, but there are other seemingly alien craft out there to be discovered. For centuries, reports have come in about strange craft below the surface of the water: Unidentified Submersible Objects.

Just as with UFOs, there are USO hotspots in the world as well. In one now-famous 1967 case in Shag Harbour, Nova Scotia, a craft reported to be 60 feet long with flashing orange lights was seen hovering over the water before tilting 45 degrees and slicing into and under the ocean. Both the police and Canadian Coast Guard were alerted, but by the time they arrived there was no sign of the craft.

Another hotspot is the waters around Los Angeles, California. And why not? Think about all of the humanity that could be observed right there: Edwards Air Force Base, with strong ties to our space program, Los Angeles International Airport—one of the largest airports in the world, Hollywood, millions of people, and deep waters just a few miles offshore: the perfect place to sit and not be detected.

You legend trippers with SCUBA diving gear and certification have yet another underwater mystery to explore (see Chapter 8, "Ancient Mystery Tripping," for more).

STARCHILD SKULL

I BEGAN THIS CHAPTER discussing the 1947 alleged crash of a UFO near Roswell, New Mexico. The reason we hold on to this story with an iron grip is because of its promise: tangible extraterrestrial evidence, in this case the wreckage that must surely still be somewhere in the world, even if it's hidden away. When someone makes a claim of abduction, either we find him believable and his story compelling or we do not. Besides his testimony, we have little else to go on.

But a crash site—now we have debris, technology, perhaps body parts—something we could hold up to the microscope and to the world.

The thirst for tangible evidence of the paranormal interacting with our world will never be fully quenched. And periodically a new piece of evidence gets entered as an exhibit into the court of public opinion. Enter the Starchild skull.

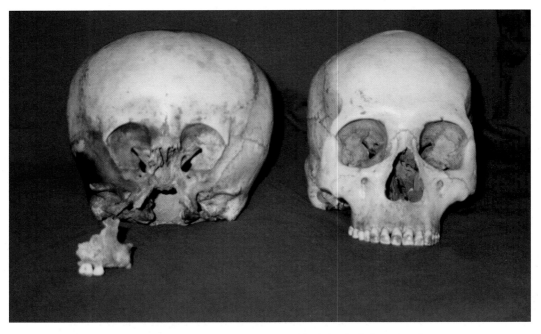

The Starchild skull next to the normal female skull found with it.
Image courtesy of Lloyd Pye.

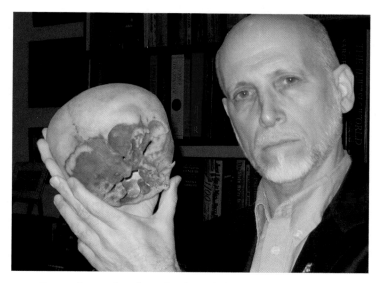

Researcher and author Lloyd Pye holds the Starchild Skull.
Image courtesy of Lloyd Pye.

In the 1930s, an El Paso, Texas, girl and her family were vacationing about 100 miles southwest of Chihuahua, Mexico, in the Copper Canyon region. The story goes that the girl went off on her own and found a cave. Inside the cave was a skeleton lying on its back next to a mound of dirt with an arm bone sticking out. The girl dug up the mound and found another skeleton with a deformed-looking head. The girl attempted to remove both skeletons and keep them for souvenirs, but she lost most of the bones in a flash flood. She was able to bring both skulls home to Texas, where she kept them in a box. The owner of the skulls died in 1990. Eight years later, the skulls made their way to Ray and Melanie Young, also of El Paso. Melanie was a neonatal nurse and didn't think the odd-shaped skull looked like any deformity she had ever seen. She wanted to find some answers, so she brought the skull to Lloyd Pye, who started the Starchild Project in February 1999 to try to find answers to the origins of this peculiar skull. I called Lloyd Pye to discuss this remarkable find. He concedes that the backstory is vague and mostly unknown.

"Early on with scientists I caught a lot of flak for it not having a good series of events that could account for where it came from," said Lloyd Pye. "It doesn't matter, it's here. You've got to deal with it. It doesn't matter how it got here, you have to confront it."

The objective of the Starchild Project is to test the hypothesis that this was a human/creature hybrid. Pye also concedes calling the skull "Starchild" was a mistake because it caused mainstream scientists to back away for fear of ridicule.

Pye's first step was to have the skull examined and X-rayed. "I had talked to enough researchers and scientists that said in their particular area they had seen nothing like this before," Pye said. "The inner ears were weird, the eyes were beyond weird, the thickness of the bone is strange, and by the end of it I was convinced it was not entirely human."

There were many skeptical scientists encountered along the way, including one who said you can stack up 10,000 physiological differences between the Starchild skull and a normal human skull, and it won't matter because nature can do anything, cause any deviation. Bring some DNA results, and maybe you'll have something there besides a birth defect.

Radio carbon dating showed both skulls to be about 900 years old (give or take 40 years). But that makes the DNA pretty old by modern testing standards. The bone of the Starchild skull is half as thick and weighs about half as much as a normal human skull, yet it appears to be twice as durable. The DNA extraction produced mitochondrial DNA, which easily proved this creature had a human mother. However, no nuclear DNA could be recovered, meaning that for years the father of this creature could not be determined. DNA testing has come a long way since 2000. The human genome has been cracked, and advanced testing procedures have allowed scientists to extract strings that couldn't be touched a decade ago.

Two more DNA tests were conducted, the most recent in 2009, and this time the nuclear DNA was successfully extracted. The result: a non-human father. Not only that, the nuclear DNA doesn't match any known species. Genetic testing also proved that the normal human skull found next to the Starchild skull is female and not a genetic match with the Starchild, meaning her egg was not used—though you're free to speculate if she was some kind of surrogate carrier.

We know on Earth that you can cross-breed some disparate species. For example, a mule is the result of breeding a male donkey with a female horse. The resulting mule is almost always sterile. These two species are close enough that the egg can grow into a viable animal, be born, and live.

Rob, Matt, and Sarah gaze skyward in search of UFOs.

How to Conduct a Sky Watch

STEP 1: Go outside where you have a clear view of the sky.

STEP 2: Tilt your head back about 45 degrees.

STEP 3: Enjoy!

Sure, that's the technical way to do it, but Rob and Sarah prefer the zero-gravity chair and a six-pack—'cause that's just how they roll.

So this unknown father species of the Starchild must be a close genetic match, right? You'd think so, but not so in this case, said Pye.

"I don't think the Starchild is a product of sexual reproduction," Pye said. "To say that this is a product of genetic engineering 900 years ago, that's where mainstream science is going to throw a wall up. But I don't see any way that this is doable other than genetic engineering."

Pye points out that the genetic difference between a human and a chimp is only about 3%. The genetic difference between a human and an ape is only about 5%. The researchers and geneticists Pye is working with believe there could be as much as a 20% to 30% genetic difference between the Starchild's nuclear DNA and that of a human.

The Starchild was alive at one point. This is not the skull of a fetus. It has teeth and had lived at least a few years before dying. The kind of genetic engineering required to create this creature is highly advanced, leading many to believe that this is a byproduct of some advanced civilization.

This legend-tripping mystery gives us something to hold on to and test: a tangible skull. The results are shaking everything we thought we knew. The Starchild skull will undoubtedly lead to more questions: Could there be another somewhere, or was this the only hybrid test case, 900 years ago? Was there a visitation? Can we find strains of this newly discovered nuclear DNA in people living today? We should all keep asking questions and keep finding answers.

Investigating the Claims

The Mutual UFO Network (MUFON: www.mufon.com)—the largest civilian task force dedicated to the study of UFOs—has an entire training program dedicated to the investigation of UFO claims. To become a field investigator for MUFON, you need to:

► Be a MUFON member in good standing.

► Purchase a copy of the MUFON Field Investigator Manual/DVDs.

► Take an "open book" test and mail the results to MUFON headquarters for grading. Those with a grade of 80% of higher are promoted to "field investigator" status.

► It's recommended that you accompany a seasoned field investigator before you attempt your own investigation.

What MUFON is trying to do is a very good thing. They want data collected in a consistent way so they can learn something overall about the UFO phenomena. The challenge is to place a myriad of human experiences into rows and columns—something I'm not sure is possible. However, I do believe legend trippers can learn something from MUFON's methods.

For help understanding how MUFON investigates an alleged UFO encounter, I spoke with Chuck Reever, Director of Investigations for MUFON International. He revised their field manual back in 2007, but as he discusses the revision, it sounds like a process that will go on forever. MUFON is very much about process, hierarchy, and data. The goal is to catalog and categorize.

"We have three areas of investigation," Reever says. "We have the general subject of UFOs, but we also have an abduction specialist, a cattle mutilation specialist, and a crop circle advisor."

Reever goes on to discuss the many categories and subcategories of experience classifications. There are fly-bys, maneuvers, anomalous lights, and close encounters. Each of these categories has subcategories.

I struggle with trying to turn a human experience into a category because two different people can witness the exact same phenomenon and reach two different conclusions. One witness might be frightened, while the other might think it was simply a cool thing to see.

Reever describes how MUFON deals with an incoming claim. The first step is for an investigator to make a personal contact over the phone to discuss what happened. This is to verify it's a real person, that he doesn't seem to be hoaxing, and that he seems to be sane. Based on the phone call, forms might be sent for the witness to fill out, depending on the specific experience.

In some cases, a field investigator might go to the location to investigate personally, or possibly the sighting will just be filed. For the cases that don't involve a psychological impact, forms may be enough. With more profound examples such as an abduction claim or some kind of contact, the investigator will go out for a face-to-face interview. He'll ask the witness to sign a form swearing to his account. Is it legally binding? No, but when someone signs his name to a form, it often carries more weight.

"I don't believe in the hard interview," Reever says. "I don't believe in the Dragnet thing…I want to do the soft interview. I want people to open up."

Reever discusses the MUFON investigation process. He speaks of people who only want to work on the big cases. That's understandable—nothing like high profiles to get people excited—but he believes investigation skills are perishable. If you don't continue to use them, they go bad. He said, "If you don't do the little things as you go along, to continually hone, to continually think about what you're doing and the information you need, you're going to forget the big things, and the little things on a big case."

Protocol and process come up again and again in our discussion. Reever speculates that 70% of cases MUFON receives have a natural/normal explanation. The other 30% just aren't known, and maybe 8 to 10% of that 30% might be alien, but he concedes that "there's no way to tell the difference" between an advanced secret human military craft and some extraterrestrial.

"We never say anything is alien because there's no way to prove that," Reever says. "But we want to know what is not identified because, over a period of time, with the database we have, we can do some correlations."

So who in the United States Government knows what we have and what's come from far away? Reever said, "I'm am absolutely convinced that there's a portion of this government [United States] that has the knowledge of what we have, but it's so compartmentalized that they don't really know where everything is. The reason for that is they've taken this technology when they've gotten it and they've put it out in the private industry. And there's another reason for that—they don't have to work with freedom of information requests. They don't have it anymore, it's gone. And when private industry gets this stuff, I think it goes so deep nobody knows what they have. Everybody's expecting the government to come out and give revelations of all that's gone on. They can't. They don't know."

Reever is driven in this pursuit because it's an intellectual exercise. This is his quest for a big truth.

Organizations like MUFON are just one direction to go with UFO tripping. You can enjoy the story, the experience, and the skywatch, or you can take the courses and delve into the database. As with all legends, take them as deep or as shallow as you're willing to swim.

UFOs captivate us because it raises the question: Are we alone in the universe? It's an important question, indeed. There's often physical evidence present, such as crop circles, scorched earth, or eyewitnesses, and the sky is almost always available for viewing somewhere. Eyewitnesses are often highly credible people: airline pilots, police officers, military personnel—people who have training and reason to be outside observing. The credibility of the source makes these legends even bigger.

You night owl legend trippers can stay up late gazing at the stars with binoculars or telescopes, but plenty of UFO sightings occur during daylight hours, too. Keep your camera poised and your eyes to the sky!

BECOMING A MAGNET

By reading this book, you're already becoming more of a magnet for legends. You're becoming more familiar with what legends look like, sound like, and even feel like. As you put your face forward and tell others what you're looking for, other people will hear about you and seek *you* out to tell you of their encounters. Embrace the reputation. Be proud to be a legend tripper. The longer you do this, the more legends will come your way.

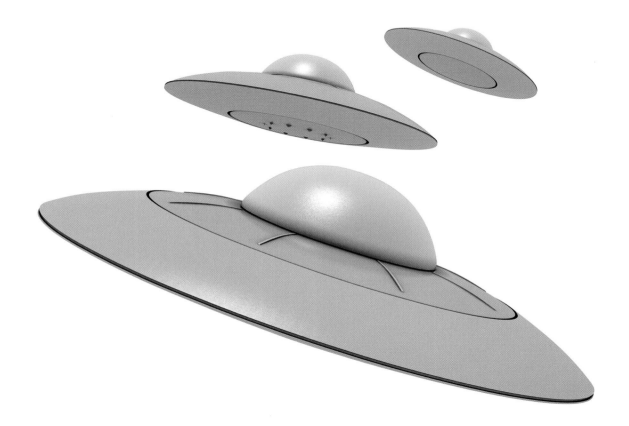

Urban Legend
Tripping

*"No... it is true. My brother's former
roommate's boss's uncle said he
knows a guy who saw it happen."*

—Anonymous

HERE'S A DARE FOR YOU to try at home. If you have a room without any windows (like a bathroom), grab a candle, some matches, and head in there. You'll need complete darkness for this one. Light the candle and hold it in front of the mirror. Now close the door and turn out all the lights. You might even want to lay a towel in front of the door to block out as much light as possible. Ready? Okay, take a deep breath and hold the candle so you can see your face in the mirror. Now start chanting: "Bloody Mary, Bloody Mary, Bloody Mary." Keep chanting. You may just summon Mary Worth.

A POPULAR VERSION OF THE STORY

Many years ago, a beautiful young woman named Mary Worth suffered a horrible accident that left her face completely disfigured. Her family feared she wouldn't be able to handle the sight of her own reflection, so they hid all of the mirrors in the house. One day Mary's curiosity got the better of her, and she went looking for a mirror. When she uncovered a hidden looking glass and saw the face before her, she screamed in horror. She wanted her old image back so badly that she walked into the mirror to search for it and vowed to attack and disfigure anyone who should ever go looking for her.

Back to your chanting. This attempt at summoning Mary has been practiced at many a teenage sleepover. You can search the Web to find examples of people claiming something happened during the chanting. One teenage girl said she and a group of friends stood before the mirror and when they said "Bloody Mary" the seventh time, the girl closest to the mirror started screaming. The scream drew the attention of Mom who opened the door and turned on the lights. They found the screaming girl huddled in the corner with fingernail scratches running down her face and blood dripping from her fresh wounds.

That's just one account; there are many others. Spend an evening reading some of these accounts before attempting your own summoning of Mary Worth. Though none of us would expect anything to happen, I defy you to tell me it didn't at least

Sarah attempts to summon Bloody Mary in the mirror.

cross your mind that you might see a disfigured face coming toward you from the other side. These stories are powerful and touch nerves deep inside of us.

The Bloody Mary urban legend has been around since roughly the 1960s, but it speaks to issues that date back centuries. The "sin" of vanity, of loving one's reflection too much, of summoning spirits, and exacting revenge on the innocent all hover over the Bloody Mary legend like a morning fog.

The mirror is a funny thing. Its image is a backward and flattened view of reality. It's a distortion. Gaze long into the abyss, and the abyss will gaze back at you—to borrow a phrase from Nietzsche. Think of the Gypsy fortuneteller staring into the crystal ball, think of the Oracle at Delphi gazing into the shiny bowl of water. Both claimed to receive images from beyond. One reason could be a simple trick of the way our eyes function.

Do you know those 3D picture albums you see at the mall? The colorful designs look like a mess until you stare at the center of the picture and then slowly move the picture away from your gaze. Then you see a three-dimensional image of a sailboat or some other picture. The reason it works is that you're fixing the focus of your eyes at an imaginary point beyond the plane of the paper. By looking past, the image appears three-dimensional. In mirror gazing you're doing something similar. You're focusing beyond the glass of the mirror. You may just see something—a hallucination, if you will—within the glass. And if you're thinking about a disfigured girl at the time, maybe your brain will manufacture something from a nightmare. Maybe. Or maybe the gaze and candle are allowing you to alter your mental state to be receptive to some kind of communication.

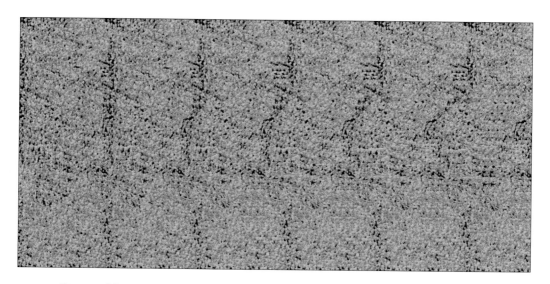

Stare at this stereogram image, focusing on a point beyond the plane of the paper.
Only when you can focus on that imagined point can the three-dimensional shark be seen.
"Random Dot Shark" by Fred Hsu.

Here's the scary reality of Bloody Mary: *Something* is happening. You can dismiss this whole thing as nonsense, as something teenagers do to scare themselves at sleepovers, but here's the problem: Bloody Mary doesn't go away. If you owned an old radio and tried to turn it on every day for 50 consecutive days, and each day the radio failed to work, there's a good chance you would quit trying to turn the radio on (you would likely give up well before the fiftieth attempt). You might try to get the radio repaired or just throw it away. But *what if* the radio worked two or three times out of your 50 attempts? You might just figure something is going on here. Why does this radio work some of the time? Maybe I should hold on to it, because there's something there.

It's the same with Bloody Mary. Something is happening somewhere that we collectively hold on to her and keep trying to summon her in the mirror. If for no other reason, we need to consider the possibility of Bloody Mary.

In this chapter we're going to celebrate and explore many of these urban legends that have wormed their way into popular culture, movies, and modern folklore.

First, we need to define the difference between an urban legend and folklore. An urban legend often has nothing to do with a city setting, thus insiders prefer to call these stories "contemporary legends." But the formula *is* agreed upon: It's a popular story alleged to be true that is spread from one person to another either orally or in writing.

REMEMBER THE TELEPHONE GAME?

Everyone would sit in a horseshoe, and the teacher would whisper a sentence to a person at one end. The sentence could be: "There are clouds moving over the mountain; it looks like rain." Each kid would whisper what he heard to the person next to them and so on until it went all the way around the room. Then the last person would say what the message is: "Mounds on the mountain are really trains." Everyone would have a good laugh as the teacher read the original sentence. The moral was usually: Don't spread stories." Those who pooh-pooh legends use this time and again as an example of why we can't trust folklore, but that's not entirely fair.

Urban legends have another dynamic: The magic lies in the telling of the tale. Here's where I depart from some folklorists. I believe that in many cases, the teller believes the story he is telling. He must, because it's the only way he can retell the story with conviction. So the teller uses his skill as a storyteller to try to convince the audience, whether the audience is one person or 50 at a time. To add credence to the story, the teller gives enough facts to make it sound verifiable, but not too many. For example, the source of the story is close but not too close, like: "my brother's girlfriend told me." The timeline is recent, but not too recent, like "about four years ago" (spring, summer, fall, winter? We don't know). And the location is real, maybe even close by: "It happened in the woods near the park on the north side of Springfield." From there the teller must keep a straight face, show that she was so moved by the story that she gets visibly shaken during parts of the retelling, and then usually offer some kind of moral to the story, like: "so be careful, because this could happen to you, too."

So, legend tripper, how do you tackle urban legends like these? We're going to take urban legends to a new level by documenting them. We'll try them ourselves, because we need to roll up our sleeves if we're going to understand what we study. But here's the new level: Document your own attempts and experiences, but also document the stories of others. Grab your audio recorder or video camera and interview people who have had experiences (or no experience). Do you have a friend who said, "Oh yeah, Bloody Mary—I remember trying that at a sleepover"? Ask if you can interview her! But here's the trick: Ask as few questions as possible. You've heard one version of the story here, but there are others floating around. Ask your friend what she knows about the Bloody Mary legend. Have her retell it in its entirety.

Settings such as a campfire lend themselves to storytelling and legend sharing.

Sometimes you have to ask the same question in a different way two or three times to get all of the details. Just nod and listen. Record everything. You may find new variations in the story that you never knew. These variants might eventually become a mainstay of the legend, but we'll never know without documenting what we hear.

Imagine the audio logs you can create with these interviews, or CDs pieced together with dozens of interviews with friends, neighbors, and colleagues about various legends. It's those stories that bind us together. What a great thing to listen to in the car or on a plane. What a great gift for all involved!

IF IT POPS, IT ROCKS

MORE SPECIFICS. I'm a child of the '80s. No apology. I have my parachute pants in a drawer somewhere, and if the Flock of Seagulls haircut ever comes back in style, I have a can of hair mousse ready and know how to get that flip going with a brush and curling iron (oh dear... I've said too much...too late now). So there I was, age 10 and in the convenience store blowing my hard-earned allowance on candy. One of my personal faves was Pop Rocks. Remember that candy? It came in a pack, you put them on your tongue, and they popped and fizzed like battery acid. Loved it!

An urban legend soon started circulating that if you ate Pop Rocks and drank carbonated soda at the same time, the Pop Rocks would explode in your stomach and kill you! To add credence to the story, people said that John Gilchrist, Jr.— much better known as "Mikey," the kid who "liked it" in Life breakfast cereal commercials in the 1970s—had died by combining Pop Rocks and soda.

Ahhh, Pop Rocks—you can still buy them, thankfully.

That's all we knew as my childhood friends ripped open a pack of Pop Rocks and then popped the top off a can of soda and slid both across the table toward me. Sweat was building up under my skin. I mean, could this be true? Am I about to do the equivalent of putting a loaded gun to my head? And poor Mikey...I mean he was just a kid. "No thanks, guys. I-I-I'm not really hungry right now."

It turns out that John Gilchrist, Jr., is still alive and well and had no such incident. And I may have tried this experiment once or twice along the way. In fact, be sure to watch the DVD included with this book as we explore this legend thoroughly.

Many folklorists like to place every legend in some kind of basket. This is understandable, and it's also very human. It's the reason we find faces in the clouds and why we hear our name being called in the wind rustling through forest trees. Many folklorists believe there are archetypal stories like the phantom hitchhiker (which we explored in Chapter 2, "Ghost Tripping"), or the rite-of-passage that Bloody Mary offers, and I would agree to a certain extent that as people tell these friend-of-a-friend tales, they are falling into categories. But this logic starts to fall apart when a person says, "I witnessed this event." He didn't hear about it from someone else, he had the experience first-hand. That's different and deserves closer attention.

THE HOOK

"THE HOOK" LEGEND HAS BEEN DONE so many times around campfires, in movies, and in other books that I must beg your forgiveness for repeating it again here, but there is so much this story has to teach us about urban legends that it bears repeating. There are so many versions of the story that I'm going to give you my own version off the top of my head. Join me in a nighttime car ride to a desolate road.

Two young lovers are out for a nighttime drive and pull over along a lonely stretch of dark road. No other headlights can be seen, and it's the perfect spot to "park" and try and find some paradise by the dashboard light. The radio is playing something romantic, like "Breakin' the Law" by Judas Priest, when the news interrupts.

"We interrupt this program to bring you an important news bulletin," the announcer says. "A homicidal maniac has escaped from the Happy Acres Lunatic Asylum and is on the loose."

"Oh my, I'm scared," says the young coed in the car. "Didn't we pass that asylum just down the road?" The driver puts his arm around her and his hopes spring even higher.

The announcer continues, "The maniac is easily identifiable because he has a sharp hook in place of his right hand. If you spot him, do not approach him. Contact authorities immediately."

Our roadside Romeo slides even closer to his date and makes his move. But she wants none of it. "Take your hands off of me and put them back on the steering wheel," she says. "I don't like being out here."

Suddenly they hear a scratching noise just outside of the car. The young girl screams, "Take me home now!"

The frustrated young man starts the car and speeds away. As the couple rolls back into town, the girl is calm. When they pull into her driveway, the gentleman gets out to open her door but screams in horror as he sees a hook and bloody stump stuck in the passenger door handle.

This story has been around so many times that few dare to tell it because we've all heard it, and even if it were true, no one would believe it because it's become a staple, or rather a cliché. But The Hook allows us to explore other facets of an urban legend. First, like most urban legends, this one has a moral: Parking is not a wholesome activity. Had the young lady not resisted her date's sexual advances, then both would be dead at the *hand* of the maniac. They shouldn't have been out there in the first place, but her prudence saved them before it was too late.

The story also has quasi-specific references to a legitimate setting. The location was in the vicinity of the Happy Acres Lunatic Asylum (replace this name with the asylum near you), and the song identified on the radio lets you know this took place in the somewhat recent past.

There's another aspect to these scary stories that many people miss: the monster/ghost/maniac as an aphrodisiac. No, really! Right after World War II, the United States entered an unprecedented period of prosperity, riding on the back of cheap petroleum. Two cars were in every garage, and GIs were back home and wanting to find some private time with their best girl.

Parking became all the rage. Find a nice desolate spot, tell your sweetie that it was right here that the ghost is said to walk or the maniac lurks, and she gets nervous and moves closer for protection (of course both are playing a role here and have equal interest in the final objective). Who would have thought that these legends could be so versatile!

Here's your task, urban legend tripper. Don't be afraid to go parking with your sweetie and see how these stories fare in the car.

If you do find yourself on the receiving end of The Hook story, break out your audio recorder. You might learn something if you can grab the subtleties from a somewhat convincing teller. If the teller is especially convincing, you might consider asking for specifics and dates. You can always check local newspaper archives to see if any facts match up. You never know, you may find the beginning of a legend—and that is quite an accomplishment in our line of work.

If your town has a specific road or quiet place where people go to park and also has a legend, do some digging. Today the story may be that a demonic ghost comes out of the woods to attack you for parking in that spot, but your research may uncover an event that took place in that location. What if there was a murder or untimely death in the vicinity? What if you can't find any legends about that area prior to that death or murder? You just discovered the legend's birthday, and you can trace its evolution! It's an incredible opportunity. But legend tripping will take it one step further: What if there's more to it than just a story? It's worth a late-night vigil in the area.

WHERE THE HELL IS MY KIDNEY?

THIS LEGEND GAINED A LOT of attention in the 1990s. The story goes something like this:

> A gentleman traveling on business in Chicago went to the hotel bar one night to blow off some steam. A seductive woman approached him, and the two shared several drinks together. Soon, the gentleman is quite inebriated, even more than usual—as if someone slipped something into his drink. That's when his female companion asks him to take her to his room for the night. The two go upstairs and fumble with the hotel room door, and then everything goes black for him.
>
> When he wakes up, his back is sore and covered in an ice pack. He feels stitches on his back and sees there's still a little blood on the sheets. Doctors soon verify to his horror that he has had a kidney removed, and it is likely for sale on the black market.

You can only hope that a doctor who would steal your kidney wears a surgical mask.

This legend has gone international since, and though the details change slightly, the gist is the same: Don't talk to strangers when traveling on business. It's legends like this that can be fueled and supercharged by just one case in the newspapers. But alas, so far there's no legit claim of theft.

Though the reason may be bunk, this legend is real and has caused enough real fear that the National Kidney Foundation (www.kidney.org) on its Web site FAQs addresses this concern, and I quote:

> What about that man who went to a party and woke up in a bathtub full of ice with one of his kidneys stolen?
>
> This is a myth that began over 10 years ago. There is no documented case of this ever happening in the United States.

Hmmm... "in the United States." Does that mean it's happened in other countries? The legend lives on.

TOUCHED BY AN ANGEL

FOR CENTURIES THERE HAVE been count-
less stories of divine intervention in the lives of
everyday people. In the realm of ghosts, I've
received at least a dozen accounts over the years
from soldiers who had a story of a comrade who
saved their neck, only to learn that this comrade
died the day before. One World War II veteran
wrote to me, telling me his sergeant burst into a
bombed-out building that he and several other
soldiers were sleeping in. The sergeant was
familiar to these soldiers and told them they had
to get up and out right now. The soldiers were
upset because they were finally getting some
much-needed rest, but they did as ordered. Once
they got outside and joined the rest of their
platoon, a bomb landed right where they were
sleeping. When one of the soldiers commented,
"It was lucky the sergeant came in and told us
to get out," he was informed that couldn't be
because the sergeant had been killed earlier that
afternoon.

In a civilian version of this story, a car with a
family of four inside goes over an embankment
in the road. The driver/dad crawls up to the road
and flags down a passing car and informs them
that he needs help—his family is stuck in the car
below. Rescuers quickly come to the scene and
are able to save the mother and two children.
When the driver who pulled over laments, "Thank
God I saw the driver on the road and could get
them help," rescuers tell him he couldn't have
seen the driver because he died on impact.

Many people interpret these experiences as quasi-
religious (something we'll delve into deeper in
Chapter 9, "Religious Tripping"). These stories
fulfill two needs: one, that our spirit lives on and
can influence and help those we care about; and
two, we need to believe in miracles, because when
all hope is lost, these stories offer us a chance.

For believers, these tales are a validation of faith
and further evidence in the supernatural. Belief
itself makes these tales more than just stories.

NOT JUST STORIES!

THOUGH WE'RE DISCUSSING these urban legends as if they're just made-up stories, don't make the mistake of dismissing this pursuit as pure fiction. Legends survive (and sometimes thrive) because there's an element to them that rings true to many people.

The reason we retell urban legends is because we suspect there's more to the story.

If I were to tell you that this morning for breakfast I had yogurt and juice, you might stand there waiting for me to say something more. It would probably get awkward, too. "Hey, that's great, Jeff," you might say, and, "My cat's breath smells like cat food."

The information is *not* interesting, and you wouldn't feel compelled to repeat it to anyone else.

If I were to tell you that this morning I went for a walk in the woods and saw Bigfoot, the Loch Ness Monster, Elvis, and a Chupacabra all square dancing in a clearing, you might slowly back away from me until you felt it was safe to turn around and run for it. You wouldn't pass on what I said because it's too unbelievable (even coming from a guy like me).

But what if I told you that this morning I had breakfast at a diner in Concord, Massachusetts, across the street from a field where a Revolutionary War battle took place in 1776, and I saw a British Redcoat run by the window. I yelled out to the owner of the diner, "Hey, did you see that Redcoat? Is there a reenactment going on today?" And the owner replied, "There's no reenactment, and I just looked down the sidewalk, there's nobody there. Hey, look at the calendar—today is actually the anniversary of the battle." Well...you might find that interesting enough to pass along. That legend may get some legs and start walking. (This didn't happen, for the record, it's just an example.)

Urban legends are fun to collect. Fill your journal with every one you hear, then note the deviations and different versions you come across. Each region has its own version of these legends, and each legend is a real thing unto itself and may just have real historic facts or evidence to support its existence.

TIP

If someone wants to tell you a legend, be sure to record it on your audio recorder or video camera. You don't want to generalize when it comes to the study of urban legends. Get the transcript of the story and capture the way the teller tells it.

MARCH OFF OF THE PENGUINS

I CALLED MY FRIEND, fellow author, legend tripper, and folklorist Christopher Balzano to ask him about his favorite urban legend. He didn't hesitate to mention "the autistic penguin."
The what?

Balzano explained that there have been reports all over the country of autistic children (or children with Downs syndrome) taking penguins out of city aquariums. He said he first heard about this legend being tied to the New England Aquarium in Boston, Massachusetts. The story goes that a mother takes her autistic son to the aquarium for the day. At some point during the visit, she loses him. She begins searching, and her frustration grows. Finally she finds her son. Upset that he wandered away, mom tells her son it's time to go home. As soon as they get home, mom sends her son to his room. After a short while of silence —too much silence—mother's intuition kicks in, and she goes to check on him. That's when she hears splashing in the bathtub. She looks in to find a penguin in her tub! That's when mom realizes that her son must have jumped the fence, waded through the water, abducted a penguin, and smuggled the bird out in his backpack.

"Why I like this urban legend is because it's actually caused aquariums to hold press conferences," Balzano said. "The New England Aquarium had a press conference to dispel this rumor. The legend forced the corporate world to react. This happened at several other aquariums, I believe one in Memphis, and one in Texas, where they had to do the same thing—hold a press conference to dispel the rumor."

Was this penguin stolen from an aquarium? Not likely.

When Balzano first heard about this legend from a friend, he called the New England Aquarium to inquire. Balzano said, "I called them and said, 'I have sort of an odd question.' The woman on the phone said, 'There are no autistic children stealing penguins, all of our penguins are here.' I mean without me even saying what I was calling about!"

So why penguins? Why autistic children? Balzano noticed whenever there's a penguin movie, or when penguins are in the news in a big way, this legend gets born anew. "When I heard about it, it was because it was in a cycle due to the movie *March of the Penguins*," Balzano said.

Besides thinking about those cute, flightless birds that always look so formal, a legend like this one promotes a bigger discussion about an unrelated subject: autism. "This goes into a deeper discussion about society's misunderstanding of autism," Balzano said. "When legends really speak to a generalization of American people, that's when it takes on more power for me."

It turns out this legend is not an American invention. The earliest version of this story appears in the United Kingdom but follows the same path: A child sneaks into a penguin habitat at some kind of a zoo or aquarium and smuggles the animal out in a backpack. Over time the legend flew across the Atlantic and landed in America (making penguins everywhere jealous because they can't even fly to the next rock, let alone across an ocean).

But this story really isn't about penguins. It's about people. It always comes back to people.

DEATH

BESIDES TAXES, IT'S LIFE'S only other guarantee: You're gonna die. We shouldn't be surprised that so many people have a fascination with death, dying, and what comes next, considering we're all going to croak. But there's another factor to legend tripping besides looking for the hereafter: putting yourself in danger...maybe even mortal danger. Let's face it, compared to our ancestors of just a few centuries ago, we're kind of soft. Humans used to have to live off the land, and their one and only occupation was staying alive another day.

Today, we go to the grocery store for food, not on a life-or-death hunt, but perhaps that primal need is still inside of us. Maybe that's why we want to park our cars in the field next to a site where locals talk about an unsolved murder where the killer is still on the loose, stalking teenagers in their cars. Could it be that the lack of real-life danger forces us to put ourselves in a different kind of danger—a place where monsters might attack us, or where demons lurk, or aliens? The need for adventure is in all of us. But for legend trippers, that need is a hunger that simply must be fed regularly.

Warning!

Anyone who reads this book will die!   Yes, it's true. All of us die. Tough break.

THE GRAVE THAT KNOCKS BACK

SARAH COOMBS, a friend, oddball, and one of the models you've seen in pictures throughout this book, recounted one of her earliest legend trips as a kid. She claims this trip is part of what led to her interest in the paranormal.

An above-ground grave in Idaho Falls, Idaho that's said to knock back at those who dare rap on the outside.
Photo courtesy of Sarah Coombs.

Sarah grew up in Idaho Falls, Idaho, and relayed a legend trip she used to take to Rose Hill Cemetery:

> I was really young. A friend of mine was also into kind of just weirder things, I guess. We were kind of a rarity in Idaho. I was about eight or nine when I was poking around in this kind of stuff. And the rumor was that our friend's older brother knew about this grave that he and his friends...of course they were in Junior High/High School so it was like super cool. Well, they would go to this graveyard and there was this grave that was unique to Idaho. Out here in New England it's completely normal, but in Idaho it was really eerie to have a grave that was above ground.
>
> So the rumor was that if you went there at night, also under a full moon, God knows, all of those little things to make it spookier. But if you went out there, you could knock on it and the resident inside would knock back.

It was supposedly this female and that means she's either a witch or a vampire—you know how those stories go. It got embellished and whatnot. So of course as soon as we reached an age when our parents would let us hang out at a park by ourselves in the daytime, we went and tried to find this grave. And the only one we could find that matched that description was this kind of above-ground sort of rectangular tomb that obviously the coffin would sit in.

We tried it, (laughs) but of course in the daylight it probably wasn't going to work because it's supposed to be at night. It wasn't until we were a little bit older, like in our early teens, that we could go back at night and try it. It never worked. We like to pretend…like, *did you hear that? Maybe it worked that time. Did you hear something? No.* We never got anything.

A friend's older brother swore that this worked for them. Even to this day I've poked around a little bit on the Internet. It's still a rumor that's floating around that this still will work if you go at night to this gravesite. And at the time, I believed it.

Sarah admits she never researched the person in the above-ground tomb, but she recalls the woman's name was also "Sarah." "I always thought that was pretty cool," she said. Today the legend isn't just passed around school yards, it's also discussed on the Internet and social media sites like Twitter, MySpace, and Facebook, which helps spread these stories faster than ever.

Sarah's legend trip was a classic rite of passage. After reading her story, I defy you, if you ever find yourself in the Rose Hill Cemetery, not to seek out that grave and knock.

Fact

CEMETERIES ARE PLACES DESIGNATED FOR THE BURIAL OF THE DEAD. THEY ARE NOT NECESSARILY RELIGIOUSLY AFFILIATED.

GRAVEYARDS ARE ALSO PLACES TO BURY THE DEAD, BUT THEY'RE LOCATED IN A CHURCHYARD.

Defying Gravity and Ghostly Proof!

THIS URBAN LEGEND HAS TRAVELED quite a bit, but I mostly think it began at a railroad crossing in the southeastern part of San Antonio, Texas, on a street called Shane Road. The story goes like this:

> Back in the 1930s or '40s, a school bus full of children broke down on tracks just as a train plowed through, killing several children and the bus driver. To this day, if you put your car in neutral on or near the tracks, an unseen force will push your car over the tracks to safety. If you need further proof, you can sprinkle talcum powder or flour on your trunk and/or rear bumper, and when it's over, you will see dozens of fingerprints of the ghosts who pushed you out of harm's way so you wouldn't suffer their same fate.

Here's the kicker—it's true! Sort of. Unless you're one of those people who obsess about their vehicle's cleanliness, then I invite you to grab some talcum powder or flour and go sprinkle it on the back of your car right now. Go ahead! I'll wait for you to get back.

I sprinkle talcum powder on the trunk of my car to see if any ghostly fingerprints will show up.

Done? Great, now wait a few minutes and go look again. You will probably see dozens of little fingerprints all over your bumper and trunk. But these aren't the prints of ghosts, these are the prints of you and your family—the people who open and close your trunk over and over, leaving oily prints on the paint that can't be seen until the fine powder soaks up the oil and displays your fingerprints.

As for the car rolling off the tracks to safety, this is a case of an optical illusion. There is a slight dip in the road that will cause a vehicle to roll forward and over the tracks. It's not obvious at first glance, so the legend survives and grows.

This legend has spread around the country; most often it's labeled "Gravity Hill." There's one in New Jersey, I know of two in Massachusetts, all with similar back stories—children died, and now they protect motorists. The kicker with this story is that I can find no record of a bus accident or any other kind of fatality at this railroad crossing. Yet the legend lives and thrives because of the physical evidence left by the talcum powder on the trunk.

Invent a legend on your own street. At your next neighborhood barbecue, tell your friends the story of the child who died in front of the house of a neighbor you don't particularly care for (this assignment works only in neighborhoods that have been around a few decades). Tell your neighbors if they park the car in front of the house, the ghost of the child who died will push on the car with all of his might to try to move the vehicle from the hallowed ground beneath.

To help build your legend, shake your head and say, "Poor little Johnny Judd." (John is my best friend since elementary school—a real name always helps.) Be sure to mention that they have to put talcum powder on the bumper to see the ghostly fingerprints.

It's my duty to tell you to come clean after you've had a good laugh at your friends' expense. How long to wait before you come clean is entirely up to you.

These legends are more than just stories, they're a way for us to connect with each other. There's an intimacy that comes from telling another person your own view or experience with these great tales. Some provide physical evidence that makes us wonder: If this is true, then what else? What else indeed. It's why we legend trip. There are dozens of elements to all legends that are true and factual. The rest takes a bit of magic. Sometimes the magic lies in the retelling.

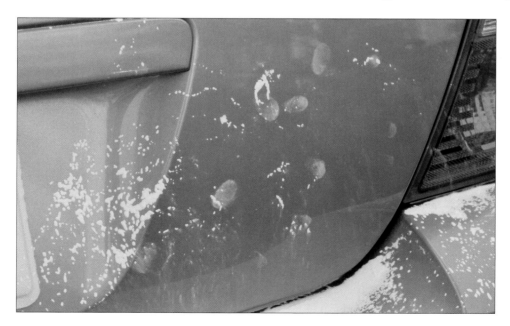

Here's what my trunk looks like after 15 minutes…notice the ghostly fingerprints!
(They look a lot like my own.)

INTERVIEWING
THE WITNESS

"In order to get the yolk of an egg,
you have to break the shell,
but if you do it with care,
the yolk will remain intact."

—Jacob Grimm

PLEASE FORGIVE THIS SHORT BREAK from legend tripping for a section on interviewing witnesses of profound experiences. I promise we'll get back to our regularly scheduled program soon, but the art of the interview deserves all the ink we can afford. There's much gold to be found as you mine these legends, but to get to that gold, you need to dig. You need to know how to interview and make your subjects comfortable enough to open up.

Interviewing tips are peppered throughout this book, but here I want to delve in a little deeper. Profound human experiences can leave a permanent mark on people. For some, it's a scar and difficult to discuss, and others find relief in the retelling, but each situation and person is unique and should be handled as such. Never assume you've heard it all, or else you stop listening.

Remember what your momma told you? "You have only one mouth but two ears, so you should listen twice as much as you talk." Time to listen to momma.

If you're legend tripping with friends, it's a good idea to break off and go solo when interviewing. Even if there are only two or three of you, it can seem like a crowd to a witness who is shy about discussing his brush with the unexplained. One-on-one you can make a personal connection before you go digging for gold.

In my career so far, I have interviewed literally thousands of people. From my days as a newspaper man speaking with everyone from celebrities to politicians to becoming a paranormal author and talk-show host interviewing experts and witnesses around the world, I've been fortunate to learn a few things about the craft of interviewing.

First, here are some tools of the trade:

Breath mints: Nobody likes funky breath. If your breath doesn't smell good, no one is going to want to spend any time with you in close proximity.

Smile: Yes, smile. Be a human being first. A genuine smile can break down walls that a jackhammer couldn't dent.

Beer: When all else fails, apply the lubricant. To quote one of the greatest philosophers of our time, Homer J. Simpson, "Mmmmm, beer." I'm not kidding here. Getting a witness to talk over a drink may yield a person who is more relaxed and open to discussing these subjects.

Breath mints, a smile, and beer—a winning combination.

Beware of people too eager to share their stories! In every situation, I'm asking myself what motivations are around me. If a person can't wait to tell me his story, I want to know why. Don't get me wrong—in some cases, people find out what I do, and they're thrilled finally to be able to talk about it with someone who won't think they're nuts. That's fair. But what about people who own haunted bars and restaurants or who want to charge admission to see the UFO landing site on their property? I don't ever want to be a part of someone's marketing plan.

The best interviews are obtained shortly after the event occurred and in private. Then the details are still fresh, and you have the best shot at documenting everything as close as possible to how it really happened.

In your interview, you need to think like a journalist. You're after *who, what, when, where,* and *why.* Feel free to also throw in *how.* Some of those questions are not answerable, but there is your roadmap for every interview. Simple, and easy to remember.

Speaking of roadmaps, write down the questions you want answered. Know ahead of time what you want to get out of this conversation. Don't wing it! That's disrespectful of your interview subject and to any potential consumers of your information. You're not bound to only the questions you write down. It's a roadmap, and you can and should take side trips, depending on how the conversation goes. Also, save the touchiest (most emotionally charged, difficult to answer, or closest to the experience you're asking about) questions for closer to the end of the interview. Once you've built some rapport, you'll get more honest and thorough answers to the tough questions.

Most of the people I interview I have never met before, which means I need to build a rapport and quickly. I start with a smile, I show genuine interest in what we're talking about (because *duh*, I *really am* interested), I introduce my audio recorder and ask permission to record so the person understands this is for the record, and then I pick my all-important lead question.

I pick my first question usually in the first few seconds of meeting a person and sizing him up. If I'm meeting a man in his 30s who is wearing a New England Patriots football jersey, my first question might be: "Hey, how do you think the Pats will do this year?" This question usually takes the person aback for just a moment before he opens up into a torrent of the value of a good defense first, then tweak the offense (or vice versa for you strike-first fans). It gets the witness talking, and that's the most important objective. My next question might be: "Did you grow up in New England?" I just took a half-step away from football, I'm still learning about the person I just met, and knowing where someone grew up helps put him into a better context.

Depending on how much time I have available, I might ask about local restaurants, or how many kids or brothers and sisters this person has. I will also share a little bit of myself. If it's a restaurant I've been to, I may comment on the food or service. I'm looking for anything we may have in common. Even tiny connections can mean a great deal. We hold on to them. I may discover we like the same music or food, and that's plenty to get me started.

When a person is leaning toward me and talking and using his hands in open gestures, I know he's feeling comfortable. Now it's time to move into my agenda/pre-written questions. It doesn't take much to lean back in toward this person and say, "So tell me what you saw in that field the other night. Is it something you've seen before or since?"

From there, you're off to the races. Make sure your audio recorder is recording!

There are two ways to guide an interview: the funnel and the reverse funnel.

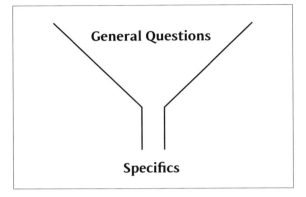

The funnel style of interview is for people who are more outgoing and easy talkers.

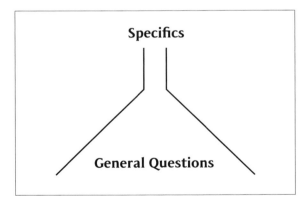

The reverse funnel style is for people who are more reserved and need specific questions to get them talking.

If I believe the interview subject is a big talker, then I start with broad questions like: "What happened?" The interviewee starts talking, and my job is to guide him down to the details, the smallest part of the funnel.

If I believe the interview subject is shy about opening up, then I start at the small end of the funnel with very specific but easy questions, such as: "Did this happen on Tuesday or Wednesday?" The shy person is less intimidated by this question because there's only one correct answer and he knows what it is. With each "easy" answer, his confidence will build, and he's more likely to open up. The more he opens up, the more we can talk about bigger stuff—like the impact this experience had on his life, what he fears, and what he cherishes.

TIP

When discussing the meat of the experience, ask the same question two or three times, spaced throughout the interview. "Counterproductive," you might say, or "The witness will think I'm not paying attention." Don't sweat it. You need to ask the big questions multiple times to fill in the details.

Here's an example. If I'm asking someone about his recent ghost encounter, it may go something like this:

ME: So what happened?

WITNESS: I was standing here and I saw this glowing figure come down the stairs. Then it was over.

That's not enough! There's always more to the story. The witness in this case rushed through and glossed over all of the details. No problem, he may still be apprehensive and worried about me judging him or his story. So I'll move on to other questions about the impression the experience left on him with follow-ups like these:

What did you think after you saw this?

Did it hit you right away or later?

Now that you've had some time to digest everything, has it changed your outlook on life or the afterlife?

These questions start to probe deep areas. You may find out about religious upbringing or spiritual beliefs. You may also learn about other factors that may influence the witness's interpretation of the event. For example, my witness above may say something like, "Well, I watch a lot of these ghost shows on television, so I know one when I see one." A statement like that will make me question the experience a bit. I can't help it. Now I'm wondering if this person is just a ghost fan yearning for his own experience. Not that the statement completely discounts the experience, but it is noteworthy.

DON'T LEAD THE WITNESS!

This bears repeating: Don't lead the witness. Come on, say it with me: Don't lead the witness! You see this in horrible television news "reporting" (those are air quotes, by the way) shows. Here are some examples of some terrible, no-good, very bad leading questions:

So this was a ghost you saw?

I bet this experience changed your opinion of life after death, huh? (Any question that ends with "huh?" is probably leading.)

So you were scared when this happened?

Any question that places your opinions or speculation on the interview subject is leading. It's also annoying to the person being interviewed, and it will skew your results no matter what. Like certain other body parts, we all have opinions. Sometimes the greatest challenge is pushing them aside and asking questions so you can get the whole story.

Back to the re-asking of questions related to the meat of a story. (You thought I'd forgotten, didn't you? D'oh! Another leading question!) I've found that the second time I ask a question about the main part of an odd experience, I tend to get the most complete answer.

ME: Let's get back to your experience when you saw the figure coming down the stairs. Can you tell me what you were doing just before it happened? What drew your attention to the stairs? Please, if you can try to slow down time and explain everything you saw, heard, felt, or even smelled.

WITNESS: I was walking to the kitchen because I heard what I thought was my wife coming through the back door. As I get near the stairs I just had this feeling… I don't know… like when you know someone else just walked in the room? You know how the air changes a little bit? For some reason I was compelled to look up the stairs, and that's when I saw something hazy—at first it was like heat rising off of a hot road in the summer—I thought maybe it was smoke and there might be a fire, so this now had my full attention. The wavy lines got more solid, like smoke forming into something, and it was moving toward me, coming down the stairs. It seemed to produce its own light somehow. Just the faintest greenish glow. It came down three or four steps. I was frozen looking at it. Then it vanished. Just gone in less than one second.

That's better. We got a lot more details that time and a more complete picture. Now that the witness is comfortable and really opening up, I can delve into more personal questions about how he feels about living in a house where something like this happened. What it means to him spiritually. If I ever get the sense that there's more to the story, I just keep asking. I rephrase questions again.

Sarah works to get Matt to open up about his recent paranormal experience.

Though I got plenty of meat when I asked about the experience the second time, I still go back for thirds. Call it cleanup. Because it's in the third telling that the witness sometimes remembers little but significant details.

ME: Anything else you can remember about that experience on the stairs?

WITNESS: No, I can't think of anything…but you know…there is one thing. Earlier that day I remember walking down the stairs and feeling really cold. I recall thinking I need to check our heat vents to make sure they're all open. I didn't really think of that until now.

I can't tell you how many times the third asking yields something interesting. If you do your job well and build a great rapport with a witness, you may get a phone call or email days later saying, "Hey, I just remembered something else." When that message comes your way, you've done well. This person trusts you with his very personal experience. Don't violate that trust. It's important.

Not violating trust means you don't use his name or location without clearing it with him first. It means you're upfront with your intentions to write about this experience in your blog, books, journal, podcast, or videos. It means you're honest. You don't need everyone to like you (though it helps if you can swing it), but you do need your credibility and honesty. In fact, it's all you have.

A few more tips to getting the gold from your witness. Silence is not only golden, it can also be very effective. If I'm interviewing a person I feel is not only holding back but might be being evasive, I may resort to the silent treatment.

It's difficult to tell when a person is being deliberate in his silence. Experience will mostly help here, but so will body language. If the witness crosses his arms before he begins to speak, he may be putting up a barrier physically as well as verbally. If he leans back and slouches before speaking, it could mean the same thing. Fight silence with more silence. Feel free to try this in social situations, too—you'll be a hit at parties (not really)!

Let's look at an example:

ME: So what happened? What did you see?

WITNESS: I saw this thing coming at me down the hall.

ME: (Silence while I continue to look at the witness with earnest interest)…(annnnd more silence)

WITNESS: (now feeling on the spot)…And I realized that this "thing" shouldn't be there. I mean it didn't have feet. I just knew something was really off.

Most people hate uncomfortable silence. They'd rather fill the empty air with words than have the maddening silence hover around them as another person watches. It takes some self-discipline to pull off the silent treatment, but it can be very effective.

Use questions like these:

> What did you feel or sense when this happened?
>
> What did you see?
>
> What did it sound like?
>
> Were there any strange smells?
>
> Did you experience any strange taste in your mouth?

Andrew's body language is closed and suggests he's not receptive to opening up right now.

Andrew's body language is leaning forward and interested. We have his full attention.

Get the witness talking, that's your primary goal. Record everything, you can sort through it later. I already mentioned capturing who, what, when, where, why, and how, but to make sure you're really getting all of the details of a human experience, ask about the senses as well.

Andrew's body language suggests he's not paying attention, he may be thinking the experience over, or he's bored. Either way, you need to bring him back to the conversation.

Remember, a good interview should feel like a conversation, because it is one. Don't take over the conversation and bear in mind your role in all of this. Think of yourself as a conductor, and the interview is the music. You have your questions in front of you, which is kind of like the sheet music, and you know where you want to go, but you must be open to some improvisation from your musician, in this case, your interview subject. And though the audience sees the conductor, the star of the show is always the musician.

The maestro is in charge, but he's not the star. Conduct, but let your musician (or in this case, interview subject), express himself.

CAN YOU TRUST A PERSON'S MEMORY?

SKEPTICS OFTEN ARGUE that memory can't be trusted. They'll cite research studies—especially related to criminal court cases—where a witness's memory turned out to be inaccurate. This is often true. I can't tell you what I had for breakfast two weeks ago on Tuesday. It's a mundane detail that my brain just hasn't held on to. I can't tell you what clothes I wore six days ago—I can take an educated guess, but I could be wrong. But when it comes to powerful emotional experiences, I remember great detail.

Where were you and what were you doing March 8, 2007? Unless that date has some meaning for you, it's likely you don't have a clue. Maybe you glance at a calendar and can say you were probably at work in your office. But you likely don't remember.

Where were you and what were you doing on the morning of September 11, 2001? That's a day many of us recall with clarity. I was sitting in an office in Westport, Connecticut. I was on the phone with a magazine advertising salesman in London who was trying to get me to buy an ad. My boss poked his head out of his office and announced a plane had just hit the World Trade Center. I figured it was a small propeller plane or something so I finished my call before heading over to his television to watch the news. As the destruction unfolded, I began to worry about my sister, who at the time worked near Wall Street in Manhattan. She was lucky to have been on a subway that stopped well short and said there was a problem and the passengers would have to go back.

9/11 was an emotionally charged day that many of us won't forget.

We can take this example to another level. When the witness is directly affected by something profound, when he feels his life is in danger, when he experiences a great deal of fear, the chemical adrenaline is released in the body. Adrenaline readies your body for fight or flight, but it also courses through your brain, first hitting the amygdala in the limbic system within the brain. This almond-shaped group of neurons is located next to the hippocampus, which is responsible for storing long-term memories.

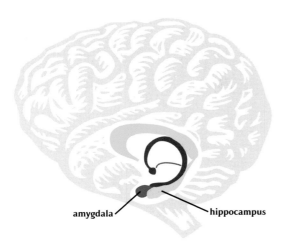

As adrenaline surges in the brain, it hits the amygdala and then the hippocampus in the limbic system of the brain in order to store the event in long-term memory.

When someone encounters a paranormal event, fear is often the first reaction because it's unknown. What is being experienced doesn't compute with how a person understands the world is supposed to work. Fear releases adrenaline, which helps burn these details into long-term memory. I trust memory when it comes to these powerful human experiences.

Matt likely won't forget this experience... if he survives.

Why is this important? Because if you were living just a few thousand years ago and found yourself walking through a dense forest when suddenly you stumbled into a hostile encampment of people who pulled out their spears upon seeing you, your life would be in danger and adrenaline would be racing through your veins. If you somehow manage to survive this ordeal, the details will be stored in your long-term memory with great clarity because it's useful information. It's data you can pass on to your offspring to make them better equipped for the future, and it's information you can use to avoid the situation next time or remember how you got out of it this time.

All we have is our powers of observation. I trust my senses, and your witness trusts hers as well.

BELIEF LANGUAGE

YOU OFTEN HEAR FROM WITNESSES of paranormal encounters that they saw/felt/experienced something indescribable. They can't seem to put into words what happened to them. This is partially due to the limitations of language. We can't always use words to express powerful emotions because they fall short of re-creating feelings this big. It's the reason there are paintings, poems, sculptures, music, dance, and all the other forms of artistic expression. The artists are trying to convey powerful emotions.

There's also a term called "belief language," first used by Hungarian folklorist Mihaly Hoppal. In Bill Ellis's book, *Aliens, Ghosts, and Cults: Legends We Live*, he describes how we use belief language to convey a paranormal event. If you use belief language improperly, you risk coming across as not believable.

Ellis's point is that it's okay in our society to say, "I think I saw a ghost last night when I was walking past the old Miller Mansion," because that puts the paranormal in the correct context. If we were to say, "I saw a ghost dipping his hand in the French fry machine at the local fast food restaurant this morning," even if it were true, it wouldn't sound true because the sentence is an improper use of belief language.

It's a quandary when legend tripping and documenting the unexplained. If we find our interview subjects believable, we want our audience to find them believable, too (because it's a reflection of the researcher as well). When in doubt, stick to the truth and the facts no matter how bizarre they may sound. Our job is to document, not to judge.

LYING? HOAXING?

WHAT IF YOUR WITNESS *IS* LYING or perpetrating some kind of hoax? This is a possible outcome of any interview; however, in my experience, liars and hoaxers account for the tiniest portion of the people I've interviewed. For one, liars most often get caught, and when they do, the court of public opinion is rather harsh on the person who fabricated the story. You may recall the three men in Georgia who called a press conference in August 2008 because they had an actual dead Sasquatch in a freezer. They even released one grainy photo to the media as "proof." This story broke all over the world, and it was covered by hundreds of newspapers and television outlets. It's worth noting how fast all of the media jumped on this story without a single reporter being allowed to view the alleged body.

I remember being thrilled for almost six seconds when I first saw the image and heard the story the day it broke. But those six seconds of euphoria soon ended when the "Wait a minute..." portion of my brain kicked in. Wait a minute... if I had Sasquatch in a freezer in *my* backyard, I would have released at least a few dozen very-high-resolution images to the media taken from every angle.

That would assure me a mile-long line of scientists and researchers who would have been at my door ready to check and verify my claim. The perpetrators of this hoax included Tom Biscardi, a self-proclaimed Bigfoot researcher who had been caught hoaxing before, a sheriff deputy named Matt Whitton, and a used car salesman named Rick Dyer. Whitton lost his job over the hoax, and Biscardi's reputation was further tarnished, and he's more or less ruined as a researcher of the unexplained. Sasquatch could move in and share a living space with Biscardi, and no one will believe him at this point. The liars have more to lose than anyone in the equation. That keeps this group to a minimum. The other way to limit this group is to try to find another witness to the phenomena if the claim sounds too good to be true.

MULTIPLE WITNESSES

WHILE LEGEND TRIPPING, there's not much more you can ask for than multiple witnesses to the same event. Not that one witness is lying or confused, but when multiple people all echo similar stories, you simply must pay more attention to what happened. The interview process for the witnesses is the same, however; each interview should be done separately first.

Listen for similarities in the stories and for the differences. Five people can all witness the same thing but remember different details.

Once all of the interviews have been conducted, try and get the group together. See what impact this experience has had. The roundtable discussion can offer insight that one-on-one interviews can't always get.

A NOTE ON INTERVIEW FORMAT

You'll notice throughout this book there are quotes and interviews from others. When I interview a person about a paranormal encounter, I print the interview as close to a transcript format as possible. You'll notice I sometimes leave in grammatical mistakes that would be unforgiveable in writing, but in spoken language we hardly notice. I might also leave in an "uhhm" or two. And I might leave in a repetition of a phrase like: "So I went down to the uhh… you know… we all went down to the cemetery." I do this because in writing about the paranormal we are often accused of sensationalizing the story. By giving the reader a transcript, I limit the possibility of my inner editor taking over. But even more than that, I want you to hear the voice of the witness if you can. I want you to know him, to understand this isn't some prepared statement being read from paper. And lastly, it's not about me, it's about the witness, so I try to keep myself out of the text as much as possible. It's a real conversation. I encourage you to use this style as you write out your legend tripping interviews.

FOR THE PROS

YOU PROS WHO WANT TO TAKE THIS to the next level: If you're attempting to document something potentially paranormal, you want as much data as possible. A witness is only as good as his credibility. If you're doing some hardcore documentation for a book or news article, you'll want to know more about your witness.

Here are the more difficult questions to ask your subject. You'll want to save these for last because you may just offend. It's fair to ask them, and if you deliver the question correctly, your subject should realize you're being thorough and have no intent to be rude.

Are you on any medications right now? (Get the list and contact a doctor to find out if they can cause any kind of hallucination or affect perception.)

Do you do any kind of recreational drugs?

Were you under the influence of any alcohol at the time?

Do you drink often?

Are you being treated for any psychological issues?

Were you under any extra stress at the time of this experience?

The objective is to rule out other possibilities. If everything seems on the up-and-up with your witness, the next step is to look around his home a bit if you can. Check out the bookshelves. What kinds of books are there? Science fiction? Paranormal books? My books (woo hoo!)? This book?

A last step is to ask for character witnesses. Spouses, neighbors, and co-workers are all good people to speak with. But respect the privacy of your interview subject, and don't offer any information that may compromise someone's ability to live in a neighborhood or work somewhere. For example, meeting a person's boss and saying, "Do you really think your employee, Jane Doe, can be trusted when she says she was abducted by aliens?" That's not going to help a situation. Be discreet, be professional.

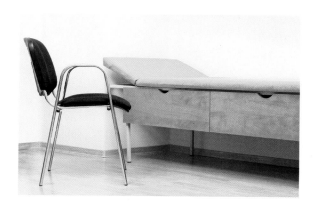

THE WRITE-UP

YOU LANDED YOUR INTERVIEWS, you've got potentially hours of audio or video tape, and now your next step is the write-up, or the edit in the case of video or audio files. Don't blow off this part. And try to get to the write-up/edit soon after the interview while it's all fresh in your mind. This will save you a ton of time. If the interview occurred in the last day or two, you'll remember most of the conversation as you hear it during the replay. If you're taking notes or transcribing quotes, you may recall, *Oh yeah, this is the part where she went on that five-minute tirade about how grocery stores don't carry the right brands anymore.* (You laugh, but it happens.) The tirade has nothing to do with the story and hopefully your recording device is blessed with a fast-forward button.

I know for some legend trippers the interview write-up feels a lot like…I don't know…work. I understand, but don't gloss over this part. When you relive your adventures again and again later on, you will want these interviews. As you reread the words, you will recall your own experience and the experience of the witness. There's an adventure to be had in the write-up, too.

Be honest and be fair with your write-up and/or editing of your interview, and you'll have a great story forever.

Now let's get back out there and do some more legend tripping.

ANCIENT
MYSTERY TRIPPING

"Mystery has its own mysteries,
and there are gods above gods.
We have ours, they have theirs.
That is what's known as infinity."

—Jean Cocteau, author and filmmaker

YOU KNOW ABOUT THE GREAT PYRAMIDS of Giza in Egypt, the Great Wall of China, Stonehenge in England, and maybe even the Nazca Lines in Peru—all incredibly ancient mysteries that force us to reconsider our ancestors' technology. But, my dear legend trippers, did you know there are probably hundreds of sites in a 100-mile radius of where you live that also have stories to tell? Did you know that archeologists may even know about some of these sites but have never come to investigate because they lack the funds and resources to look into every historic mystery that's uncovered? That's where you come in. You have the opportunity to go legend tripping through ancient times and possibly make some solid contributions to archeology.

There are locations with religious meaning, burial sites, and beliefs about the future based on ancient prophecies. The reason you heard December 21, 2012, is (or was, depending on when you're reading this) going to be the end of the world is because someone looked at the Mayan calendar, made an interpretation, and then yelled his opinions louder than the next person. There's nothing stopping any good legend tripper from learning the ancient symbols for herself, following the research, standing at the sacred site, and reaching her own conclusion. In fact, that's a big part of the point of legend tripping. We're going to study the evidence and think critically for ourselves. There's no better journey!

The Mayan calendar is renowned for its accuracy in forecasting astronomical alignments. But can it tell us when the world will end?

Here in New England near my own Legend Tripping World Headquarters (currently housed in my basement next to the kegerator), there are many stone sites. Some of them are alignment stones perched on a hillside. If you were walking through the woods and saw one of these stones, it's possible you would think it's a piece of a Colonial-era stone wall (Lord knows there are plenty of those around), but maybe those two stacks of rocks no taller than your waist are part of a set. Native Americans often set up alignment stones to signify astronomical events. If you find two stacks of rocks on a hill, there may be another single rock at the base of the hill—the idea is that you would stand behind the single rock and line it up between the two stacks of rocks at the top the same way you would line up a shot with a gun. When certain stars or maybe the moon lined up in that site, it could mark a solstice, or a harvest time, or maybe a time to migrate south for the winter.

Sites like these are sitting in fields and forests waiting for you. Jump in. We're going to photograph the site from every angle (because you don't know when kids, a construction company, or Mother Nature will come in and redecorate), measure distances, and talk to locals. We're going to find out who lived in these regions before us, we'll find out what they believed, and maybe we'll make a late-night journey back to these sites to see what happens when the moon lines up just right.

For as long as there have been humans, there have been ancient mysteries dwelling inside of our minds and souls. Call it ancient inner space tripping—where you go within for a supernatural experience.

WHAT IS CONSCIOUSNESS?

We have to start with this basic question. You may be thinking: *Jeff, I'm obviously conscious right now because I'm reading this.* Don't be so sure... did you know there's no universal agreement among scientists as to how we even define consciousness?

The loose psychological definition is that it's your individual awareness of your own personal thoughts, memories, your environment, emotions, and physical sensations. One problem with that definition is that you could be asleep in a dream state and believe you're aware of all of those same criteria even if you're dreaming that you're flying through the sky while flapping your arms. Yes, you're dreaming, but in the dream, flying is a believable reality to you.

Some define consciousness the way Freud defined the ego—a mediator among the id and super-ego and the external world. By balancing internal desires and reality, the ego shows how we view ourselves.

To some, consciousness is a river that's always flowing for each of us. Sure, little tributaries, forks, and offshoots come up now and then, and in some places the river roars like rapids and in others it's almost as still as a lake, but it continues to move forward toward some unknown destination. If you're religiously inclined, you may believe that rivers flows on to heaven; if you're an atheist, you believe eventually the river just peters out and dries up (when you die).

Tricky stuff, I know. Let me try to simplify as best I can: You know what you know, you know who you are, and you know what you experience. Let's go with that.

One of the problems with inner space tripping is that there will be plenty of people who won't believe you. Of course there's plenty who won't believe you if you say you saw a ghost, UFO, or Bigfoot, but with inner journeys it's a greater number. "You were dreaming," is one comment you'll hear. "Sounds like an overactive imagination," is another. This means you'll have to be content with the experience in and of itself, with knowing in your heart of hearts what's real and what's not for you.

There are adventures to be had inside of our minds, from dreams to astral projection. Watch for other sidebars in this chapter to take some ancient, inner journeys.

AMERICA'S STONEHENGE

IN THE SMALL TOWN OF SALEM, New Hampshire, sits a millennia-old mystery on a rocky hilltop. These old sites are perfect for a legend trip because not only are their origins a mystery, but often other phenomena have been reported in and around the location, in this case, ceremonial magic and even ghosts! A mysterious site becomes a magnet for all things unexplained.

As I embark up the trail toward the site, I pass smaller stone structures on the heavily wooded hill—they look almost like lookouts a soldier might duck behind. The construction is not complex, though the labor would be back breaking, I could probably construct something similar within a day, assuming I had another person to help me roll and lift the rocks into place and we could find enough rocks in the vicinity (this is New England, I'm sure there's plenty).

America's Stonehenge, also known as "Mystery Hill," is believed to be a 4,000-year-old calendar.

Further up the climb, I see a pre-historic fire pit and well, though there's little remaining of either, and if not for the small sign telling you what it is, I might have walked right past.

As I near the summit of the area, also known as "Mystery Hill," I see a series of stone structures sitting atop a large rock that makes the hill top look bald. When I approach the stone structures, I'm struck not by *how* humans could have created these structures so long ago but by *why?*

The stone walls and structures are built low to the ground—none are as tall as I am. Clearly there's significance to the way these structures are built—it looks too deliberate.

On my legend trip I meet the owner of the site, Dennis Stone, who runs America's Stonehenge with his wife, Pat. Dennis's father, Robert Stone, set up this place as an open air museum back in 1957. "We think it's a religious site because of the size, shape, and orientation of the structures," Dennis Stone said. "They're kind of small, so they would be kind of hard to live in. We think it might have been used for temples, especially the really small [structures]."

An alignment stone meant to be viewed from a central location. When the sun, moon, or specific stars or constellations line up with this stone at a certain time of day, it marked specific events such as a solstice.

As I walk around the hilltop, I can see trees have been cleared to reveal other stone walls that look like the Colonial walls I have in my own backyard, but in the center are very large megalithic rocks standing vertically, as if pointing skyward. At first, archeologists assumed the site was Colonial, meaning maybe two centuries ago early colonists from Europe built these stone rooms to store food or goods. But the size and locations of these stone chambers didn't make for a very good root cellar. Something seemed odd about this site.

Serious study of this location didn't begin until the 1960s. A research group soon discovered that this might be an ancient calendar—that when observed from a central point, lunar and solar positions on the rocks mark solstices and equinoxes. But the alignments are off slightly. By doing the math, the team discovered that the last time the alignments would have been accurate would have been about 4,000 years ago! We know there were people in this region well before 4,000 years ago, but archaeologists didn't think the Native Americans worked in stone—this place just isn't their style. The Native Americans in this region were more nomadic. Given the hundreds of smaller stone sites around the region, it's also shortsighted to assume that the native groups in this region never touched New England's most abundant natural resource (rocks). But something about this site was different. It looked almost Celtic in origin…like similar stone calendars in Ireland and England.

Stone said, "The solstices don't quite work today, because Earth's tilt has wobbled. We had our site professionally surveyed from 1973 to '77; we put in all of the site's coordinates and sent it off. The Harvard Smithsonian Center for Astrophysics took our computer tape and told us that around 1800 BC the alignments would work, plus or minus a century or two. And the oldest carbon dating we have of the main site is from 2000 BC. That's why we say 4,000 years old."

As I walk through the structures, I can't help but notice a large stone slab with a carved groove around the perimeter. It looks a lot like… well… a cutting board for meat that you might have in your kitchen, where the groove is designed to capture the juice. Dennis Stone said, "The table is about 9 feet by approximately 6 feet in width, it's a bell shape, and it's about a foot thick. It weighs about 4 1/2 tons. It's attached to the Oracle Chamber. If a person was on their back, by the left foot the rectangular drain goes off, and it drains right by the left foot. And there's a cutout in the bedrock where a vase could sit. You could use your imagination."

The Oracle Chamber is a small room beneath the stone slab with a tunnel coming out from under the rock about the length of my arm. When I yell into the tunnel, my voice echoes from under the slab.

Clearly this site was used for rituals, possibly human sacrifice. The site now draws many groups of people. There are those who have heard stories of strange glowing lights hovering around the site at night. Then there are Pagan people who come here to hold dances and rituals, especially during the solstice and equinox.

The sacrificial altar at America's Stonehenge.

Native Americans *did* live in this area for thousands of years. Colonists *did* live around this area a few centuries ago, and people *do* live in this area now. The origins of this site go back thousands of years, and each culture since has blended itself into this story to the point where we may never know the site's original intent, but we do know what it is today. It's a location that some call haunted, others call sacred, and others believe is an archeological curiosity.

The story and legend continue. As a legend tripper, I want to take a snapshot of where it is today. I want to speak with the people who hold ceremonial magic rituals to see if they're getting results, I want to speak with the witnesses of ghostly phenomena, but more than anything I want to walk the site, to sit in the middle of the granite hilltop, and breathe it in. And that mission was accomplished.

Is This the End of the World as We Know It?

DOOMSDAY, FINAL JUDGMENT, Check-Out Time. It goes by many names, but only one concept: Life as we know it ends. Humanity has been obsessed with our own ending for centuries. Some believed the world would end as the clock struck midnight on December 31, 1999—that the rollover to 2000 marked the end times, where airplanes would fall from the sky, and anything with a computer chip, from a blender to an elevator, would somehow explode and take us all with them. Then there's 2012 and Mayan prophecy, which I mentioned earlier. I'm convinced humankind needs to know the end is just on the horizon. It somehow makes us feel better.

There are many legend trips one can take through the history of various doomsdays that have passed, but even more interesting is how people are currently planning for the end of the world. See that guy with the wild eyes on the street corner holding the sandwich board sign reading: The End Is Nigh? Ask him why he thinks so. Don't make a joke of it, don't be a smartass. Walk up and ask him why he feels this is so. Ask to interview him, record the interview. You may learn a new theory. Remember, this *is* reality to this person—so much so that he spends his days trying to warn others. You may gain a new perspective from the interview.

And before you go thinking that only deranged street-corner folks are worried about the world ending, don't forget that governments are spending millions in preparations. Let's take a legend trip to the Island of Svalbard in Norway.

On the Norwegian island of Svalbard sits the Doomsday Seed Vault—just don't get too close, there are armed guards at the entrance to the underground vault that is now home to half a million crop seeds. And if the armed guards don't get you, the island is home to many polar bears that might look at you as their next meal.

Built into the Arctic permafrost at a cost of about $9 million, the vault stores seeds that are meant to be stored in case a natural or man-made disaster wipes out entire species of crops.

The Doomsday Seed Vault in Norway.
Photo by Mari Tefre (courtesy of Wikicommons).

The idea offers a sense of security and is also depressing. Someone (in this case the Norwegian government) saw the need to take this action at a cost of millions of dollars.

It's easy for conspiracy theorists to wonder what the Norwegian government knows that we don't know...

...and the seed vault in Svalbard isn't the only one in the world.

In the 1950s, when the "Red Scare" was in full swing, many families built bomb shelters in their yards—a place to run to when the nukes came crashing down from Russia. If someone thought about what would really happen if a nuclear weapon was detonated nearby (assuming you had enough warning to run to your shelter), an underground shelter might allow you and your family to survive the initial blast, but it might also guarantee you a slow, painful death from radiation. Nice.

But the reality is that building those structures gave some people peace of mind—they were being proactive when it came to the safety of their families. The belief gave them peace, though the reality was that in a nuclear attack, they probably wouldn't survive.

Don't fall into the trap of judging people from the past. You might say, "Oh those people in the 1950s didn't know what we know now." Not so. History repeats again and again. In February 2003, Home Depot, Lowes, and other hardware stores experienced a run on plastic and duct tape. Why? Because Americans feared a biological or chemical attack from terrorists. Some believed they could seal up their houses in the event of such an attack and that would keep their family safe... of course with a sealed up house or room, you have another problem—a finite supply of oxygen.

Preparing for the end of the world may just allow us to burn off that nervous energy. Enter the legend trip. Let's find someone who is preparing for a doomsday scenario, check out his preparations, and document why he thinks he will be spared.

WARNING...

One word of warning: With doomsday scenarios, you are treading on fragile ground. For some this is a time for spiritual readiness, and for others it's a time to stockpile guns and ammunition. Don't mock or be disrespectful of the people you're seeking. It's not fair, and it could be dangerous. Did I mention that some of them are armed?

Zzzzzzzzzzzzzzzzz

Dreaming. Each night we (hopefully) sleep. Though many people claim they don't remember their dreams, their subconscious is still hard at work during their sleep cycles. The act of sleeping isn't even fully understood! We know we need sleep, we know without sleep your immune system suffers, your attention span shortens, and eventually you can have a neurological breakdown and die.

A dream, by its definition, is a hallucination. You're seeing imagery, maybe even hearing things and feeling sensations, but it's within your mind. There are theories as to why we dream, and one is that sleeping and dreaming help us with memory storage. During sleep, your mind is sorting through the day's experiences and moving the big items into long-term memory, maybe deleting the mundane items, and placing others in short-term memory.

There's a legend that if you find yourself falling in a dream, if you hit the ground, you'll really die.

Not true.

On a more esoteric level, dreams are your subconscious communicating with your conscious mind. The language of the mind is imagery. Spoken language is learned, but imagery is imagery. Your subconscious may be using that axe-wielding monster in your nightmare to help you work through an issue you're having with a coworker.

There have been many dream dictionaries published (I even wrote one) and many attempts to assign meaning to specific images. For example, "water" tends to be tied to emotional issues, while "fire" may be an issue that is of great importance in the short term. We could go on, but there's no need.

I'd like to introduce you to the world's greatest and most accurate dream interpreter. Find a mirror... there! That's right; you are best equipped to interpret your own dreams. Let's go dream tripping.

FOR DREAM TRIPPING, YOU'LL NEED

- ☐ a notebook
- ☐ a pen

Place them next to your bed and be ready to write as soon as you wake up.

You can start dream tripping as early as tomorrow morning. As soon as you wake up, grab that notebook and pen and write down everything you remember from your dreams. Don't worry if you don't recall anything. Take a deep breath and try to remember anything, even if it's just a color you recall seeing, or just one item.

Date the journal, and write it down. Your first entry may look like this:

August 8, 2012—I recall seeing a school bus.

That's it. Not much to go on, I know, but take heart, you will get better. If you make this a daily practice, you'll find you begin to recall more and more details of your dreams.

Now for the fun part: interpretation. Your job is to line up those dreams with what's happening in your life. If you're having recurring dreams, it's an issue that you're still working through. If you're having nightmares, this is a major issue, like your subconscious screaming to get your attention.

In most cases, the images aren't obvious. But look to your own life for interpretation. Is your dream in a grocery store? If so, maybe you're having some kind of issue related to food in your life. Are you dieting? Have high cholesterol? Indigestion? Hypoglycemia? Look to your life and interpret the meaning. You'll get better at this with practice. The more you understand and remember your dreams, the more you might be able to control them, and then the real adventure begins.

Nazca Lines

In Nazca Desert in Peru, there is a series of geoglyphs, or lines that run all over the desert and on the hillsides. Archeologists believe these lines were created between 200 BC and 700 AD by the Nazca people, who lived in and around this region. What makes these lines the subject of great speculation is that many of the shapes, which include images such as monkeys, fish, a spider, birds, and a human-like figure, can only be appreciated from hundreds if not thousands of feet in the air! Other lines run as straight as runways for great distances, a fact that led author Erich von Däniken to speculate in his 1968 best-selling book *Chariots of the Gods?* that perhaps this was a runway designed by the Nazca for extraterrestrials to see from a great height—a kind of welcoming to beings from another world.

Why roll out the red carpet for an advanced civilization from a galaxy far, far away? Von Däniken postulates that these aliens were revered as gods by the native people. These "gods" came with incredible and advanced technology that promised to redeem, enhance, empower, or otherwise elevate the culture and technology of the Nazca people.

As evidence to this theory, von Däniken cited the 1930 encounter of three Australian prospectors, the Leahy brothers, when they arrived in the New Guinea highlands—an area they thought was uninhabited. What they found shocked them.

The Leahys also brought a motion picture camera and were able to capture some of the most incredible footage archeologists and sociologists had ever seen.

It turns out these highlands *were* inhabited by many thousands of aboriginal people who, though they had agricultural skills, had little else. They had never seen a white man before or anything resembling technology. The Leahys were instantly revered as gods. They looked different than any humans this group had ever seen, but more importantly, they had magic powers. They could carry fire in their pocket and produce it at will (lighters or matches). These white men also had mighty sticks of sorcery—they could point this long stick at a pig a distance away, a thunderous boom came out of one end, and the pig was dead (a rifle). These men could also call upon great silver birds from the sky to come down and carry them away (airplanes).

The Nazca Lines—ancient artwork in the sands of Peru. But what does it mean?

An ancient Candelabrum figure on a sandy hillside in Paracas National Park in Peru.

Though the Leahys may not have meant to do so, they had legions of worshipers willing to do anything these "gods" asked. Any gift the Australians offered to those who helped became sacred.

It's not a far leap to assume an extraterrestrial species with the ability to travel at great speed and distances with advanced technology might also be revered as gods—especially considering just a few centuries ago, when space travel didn't exist even in the realm of science fiction.

Some Nazca lines do look like runways. Most archeologists have dismissed any notions that these lines were meant to be observed from airborne vehicles, but the lines still raise the question.

Construction of the lines was relatively simple. The rocky soil of the desert is dark. By clearing away just a few inches, lighter sand is revealed underneath. It is believed this activity was performed by a large number of Nazca people who saw this endeavor as a communal and spiritual endeavor. The desert was their canvas, and this is what they chose to create. But what was their muse?

One of the most intriguing figures is a 100-foot-tall human-like figure with a large oval head and owl-like eyes carved into a hillside. Given the detail of the monkey and fish, it's reasonable to conclude that this figure's rounded and exaggerated shape isn't due to a lack of artistic ability. Maybe the ancient Nazca were trying to emulate something they saw. Maybe, as von Däniken writes in his book's introduction, "We have a forest of question marks." So too with legend tripping.

BERMUDA TRIANGLE

SOME LOCATIONS HAVE AN AIR of disaster around them. Like seeing a pothole up ahead in the road, you know you don't want your car to hit it, you see the hole, you know you need to move over a bit, but you still roll right into the pot hole. *Bam!* The Bermuda Triangle is the most famous 440,000-square-mile area on the planet. The triangle's points are Miami in the southern tip of Florida, San Juan, Puerto Rico in the east, and the island of Bermuda to the north.

It's known as "Hurricane Alley" for the number of big storms that pass through the region, and the waters go from very shallow to miles deep, but can those two factors explain every airplane and boat disappearance over the last several centuries? A good legend tripper looks at the stories and the data. Fortunately, there's plenty of both in the Bermuda Triangle.

Once we identify a region as being a hotspot for legends, it's natural for researchers to dig through history books to try and find other events that might add to the legend. We want to see how far back these roots go. In the Bermuda Triangle, many point to Christopher Columbus as being one of the earliest to record strange happenings in this region.

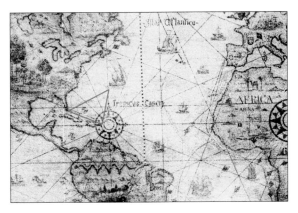

The Bermuda Triangle is the giant area that lies between Miami, San Juan, and the island of Bermuda.

In August 1492, Columbus set out on an expedition west from Spain. The mission was full of peril, and some of the crew weren't sure if they'd ever see land again. Columbus made a few log entries worth noting. One was a compass anomaly. On September 13, 1492, he wrote: "On this day at the beginning of night the compass northwested and in the morning they northeasted somewhat." On September 23, his ships were stuck in the doldrums—a region around Earth's equator where wind is scarce. He wrote: "Sea rose high and without wind." But Columbus's most intriguing log entry occurred on October 11, 1492. In the distance he saw a strange light. "...it was like a wax candle rising and falling," he wrote.

In 1840, a 22-ton French merchant ship called *Rosalie* was found drifting in the Sargasso Sea—a huge region of ocean with still waters covered with seaweed. An unmanned ship at sea is called a derelict. When another ship encounters an unmanned vessel, the rule of the sea is that the found ship becomes the salvage property of whoever finds it. When the finding party boards the unmanned ship, it's usually obvious why the crew left—maybe pirates killed the crew and took the supplies, or disease or lack of water killed the crew. But on the *Rosalie* there was nothing amiss. There were food stores, the supplies were intact, and the ship was in a good sailing state. One only abandons ship in the middle of the ocean as a last resort, so why did the *Rosalie* crew abandon her?

Columbus and the *Rosalie* are just backstory to the case that really got people wondering about this region: The disappearance of Flight 19.

On December 5, 1945, off the coast of Florida, 27 men and six TBM Avenger airplanes vanished. No wreckage and no bodies were ever found.

Just after 2:00 p.m. on December 5, 1945, flight instructor Lieutenant Charles Taylor took off from the Naval Air Station in Ft. Lauderdale, Florida, flying his TBM Avenger aircraft. Behind Lt. Taylor were four other Avenger planes flying a training mission. Four of the planes carried three men on board, and one of them only had two. The mission involved flying 56 miles east to a place called Hens and Chickens Shoals near the Bimini Islands and dropping their bombs on a practice target. Next, the planes were to continue east for another 67 miles before they turned north for 73 miles, then turn back southwest for 129 miles, completing a triangular route, and landing back in Ft. Lauderdale. That was the plan, but during the flight something went wrong.

After the five Avengers dropped their bombs, they got lost. Around 3:45 p.m., Lt. Taylor got on his radio and said to one of the other pilots in his group, "I don't know where we are. We must have gotten lost after that last turn." This transmission was picked up by Lt. Robert Cox, another flight instructor who was flying near the Ft. Lauderdale base. Lt. Cox got on his radio and asked the pilot what seemed to be the problem.

Lt. Taylor radioed back: "Both my compasses are out, and I am trying to find Ft. Lauderdale, Florida. I am over land, but it's broken. I'm sure I'm in the [Florida] Keys, but I don't know how far down and I don't know how to get to Ft. Lauderdale."

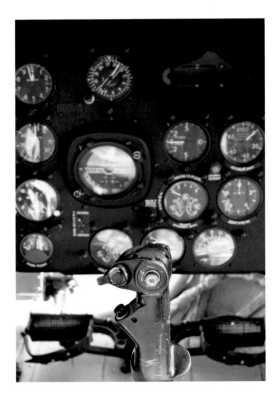

Taylor turned on his emergency beacon equipment and announced that he believed he had his bearings now. Around 5:22 p.m. a control tower reported hearing a conversation between Lt. Taylor and the other pilots in his group. Taylor announced that when one of the planes was down to ten gallons of fuel, they would all make water landings together. He radioed to base and said he would head west until he found land or ran out of fuel, but soon after he turned east again. Given that the team dropped their bombs on target well to the east of Ft. Lauderdale, no one can figure out why Taylor believed he was ever over the Gulf of Mexico during this training mission.

The Ft. Lauderdale base believed Taylor and his men had enough fuel to fly until about 7:00 p.m.. When 7:00 came and went with no sight or sound from the group, a PBM-5 Mariner seaplane took off from Banana River Naval Air Station in Palm Bay, Florida. At 7:30, the Mariner made a routine radio transmission to base and then was never heard from again. No wreckage and no bodies were ever found.

The next day a search and rescue mission yielded nothing. This incident is the most significant disappearance in Bermuda Triangle history because it's well documented, the people involved were military professionals who are supposed to know what they're doing and how to operate their equipment, and the case remains unsolved.

There have been many other cases of disappearing boats (both small and large) and airplanes before and since 1945, which is why we still talk about this mystery. With all of the pilots involved in the 1945 incident gone, we'll never truly know what happened. But some people do live to talk about what they saw in the Bermuda Triangle.

On December 4, 1970, Bruce Gernon was taxiing his Beechcraft Bonanza A36 airplane to the runway on Andros Island in the Bahamas. He was heading west to Miami, Florida, a trip that should take about one hour and 15 minutes given the clear conditions. Bruce's two passengers included his father and a friend. At 3:00 p.m., the plane took flight.

I had the opportunity to speak with Gernon about his now-famous experience on that short flight. As with any legend tripping interview, I let him talk as much as possible. I want to relive this experience with him if I can.

BRUCE GERNON

It started off with this lenticular cloud [stationary, lens-shaped cloud that usually forms at high altitudes] right off shore of Andros. When I got on top of that cloud, it was like a bubble cloud, and that spread out in the shape of a circle. It's kind of like taking a can of gasoline and making a circle with it and then igniting it at one end and then it rapidly burns to the other end. That's kind of how this type of storm forms. It's igniting right as I'm flying over the birth of it, and then it spread out, I estimate, at 300 miles an hour. And it wouldn't be a 300-mile-per-hour wind, it was a 300-mile-per-hour ignition.

This cloud lays right on the surface of the ocean, because it's probably tying in to the core of the earth for electromagnetic energy. I got free of it at 11,500 feet and then leveled off. I saw this strange cloud formation as far as I could see on either side of me for like 10 miles. This thing had spread out from one mile wide to 20 miles wide in about 10 minutes. So now I'm flying in the middle of this storm that's a giant ring around me. The diameter of this storm is like 30 miles, so when I was in the middle of it, I couldn't see either end of it anymore. But that was only for maybe a minute.

All of my instruments that are operated by electricity or magnetic instruments were malfunctioning. The altimeter is operated by barometric pressure, so it was okay. The compass was slowly spinning all by itself, and all of the electronic instruments were malfunctioning. But the radio worked.

I tried to push the plane through the clouds, but the electricity was too intense. There wasn't any precipitation, just strange electricity, strange flashes, so I turned back into the center of the ring and kept going southerly along the edges of it, and then I saw where the two ends came together there looked like what was a valley in the clouds.

On the top it was the highest cloud I've ever seen. It seemed to be 60,000 feet or more. I saw what looked like a tunnel forming through the clouds with blue sky on the other side at around 10,000 feet. I'm at 11,500 feet, so I'm able to dive down and pick up speed as the tunnel starts to close. I push the throttle and pick up all the speed I can because the tunnel is collapsing. It was exactly 3:30 when I entered the tunnel.

I was a hundred miles away from Miami, and then I came out of the tunnel, so now I'm 90 miles away from Miami. And when I came out of the tunnel the sky was perfectly blue.

When I popped out of the tunnel, that blue sky immediately disappeared to a hazy fog, and these slits opened up parallel to the direction of the flight of the airplane. Well, those slits I thought they were many miles long when they opened up. That's what I couldn't understand why in 10 seconds the fog had disappeared—there wasn't anymore fog. Three minutes later I'm over Miami Beach.

So a trip that should have taken 75 minutes took 45?

I couldn't comprehend that part for more than 30 years. How could that be possible that the sky would disappear and then reappear three minutes later over Miami? But when I came up with the theory that this electronic fog was attached to me, then everything started to make sense.

Now I believe those lines I was looking at were the fabric of time. And there was a rip of the fabric of time when I got in. Time was going forward, so I was going forward through space time while I was in the tunnel. It was pretty incredible.

The reason I didn't see the blue sky was because I wasn't flying through this fog. That's what every pilot and mariner in the past has always thought because that's the way the human mind thinks—that you're flying or travelling through this fog. You can't tell that you're not travelling through it, you're travelling with it. When I finally realized I was travelling with it, it finally made sense. Those slits weren't many miles long; they were probably only a hundred yards long or so. And the blue sky didn't disappear; I was flying through that blue sky with this fog attached to me.

Do you think this is what Flight 19 encountered?

Absolutely. Because it attached to them within 30 miles of where it attached to me. Flight 19 was 30 miles north of where I was. And it attached to Flight 19 exactly 25 years less one day earlier than me. I was the 4th of December.

Bruce Gernon is a legend tripping treasure. He's placed his story and evidence on his Web site: www.electronicfog.com. He's a person who had a profound experience and has no fear of sharing it so that we can all learn something. Bruce won't be with us forever, and neither will tens of thousands of others who have touched something amazing. Document their stories. Take it seriously. This is the gold we seek in legend tripping.

ATLANTIS

SPEAKING OF THE BERMUDA Triangle, the lost city of Atlantis—a legendary advanced culture and civilization said to have sunk into the ocean around 9600 BC—is believed to reside within the confines of the Triangle. The story of Atlantis was first told by the Greek Philosopher Plato when he described a naval power from "in front of the Pillars of Hercules" that conquered many parts of the coastal Atlantic Ocean. As the story goes, the entire country sank in a single day and night of misfortune. Today people still speculate whether this is just a story, an oral tradition, or if there is a base in fact.

One of the leading contenders for the location of Atlantis are the warm waters in the southern section of the Bermuda Triangle. One piece of evidence believers point to is an underwater feature called "Bimini Road" because it's located off of the island of North Bimini in the Bahamas. The feature rests in 5.5 meters of water, is comprised of rounded stones, and runs for almost a half mile in length.

Sea diving legend trippers have plenty to search for under the water. From shipwrecks to caves to potential archeological ruins that may have belonged to lost civilizations, there's no reason legends can live only above the surface.

I can't stress enough that you can make valuable contributions to fields of science even if you never graduated high school. Archeologists have only so many resources. If you find a location of interest, it's a mystery waiting to be solved.

Your job is to document all that you can to help pique the interest of archeologists in your region.

ASTRAL PROJECTION

Imagine being able to safely leave the confines of your physical body and travel anywhere in the universe at speeds faster than light. It's the promise of astral projection. The idea is to project your consciousness out of your body and control where you go and what you do. Those who claim to do this successfully claim they can go across town, across the state, the country, to the moon, Mars, you name it. They claim they are always attached to their physical bodies via a silver cord. And though their consciousness is away from their physical body, they claim the sense of their bodies still work. So, for example, if a fire alarm went off nearby while your astral body was traipsing about in the streets of Rome, you would instantly be pulled back into your physical body where you would wake up so you could react to the emergency.

This may sound like a fantastical dream, but the United States government took it seriously enough to study astral projection and remote viewing in something called "Stargate Project." The project was allegedly active from the 1970s to the mid 1990s, though some believe it's still going on.

Call it the ultimate spy program. The spy—in this case, a remote viewer—can sit in the safety of a bunker in the United States and project his consciousness into enemy territory and find missiles, maps, troops, and more.

Those who believe we have a body of energy and consciousness inside of us claim many of us have already experienced some degree of astral projection, but mistook it for a dream. For example, have you ever heard your bedside alarm go off in the morning, sat up groggy, and stumbled to the bathroom only to find you're back in bed with the alarm going off again? Some believe that's astral projection—your consciousness leaving your body doing your morning ritual just before your physical body actually woke up.

SOME ANCIENT SITE WORDS OF CAUTION

PLEASE DON'T DIG JUST YET! Try not to disturb the location. Take all of the photos you can, videos, and GPS coordinates, but don't put shovel to dirt. If the site has historical significance, you don't want to break anything.

If you find a peculiar site, first do your research! Find out who lived in the area, who owns the land now, and everything else you can. How? I'm glad you asked. If you find a site, here are some great places to begin your hunt for facts in ascending order:

Library local to the site: Librarians love these kind of quests. If they don't have the documents in their possession to answer your questions, they will know other resources who can help.

Local historical society or commission: This is a group sometimes funded by a town or county, sometimes comprised of volunteers. They know their regions, and if they can't get you the answers, they may know how to send you up the chain of command. At the very least, by this step you should know how long the area has been inhabited and which groups were in the area before modern people.

Regional archeological research group: There are groups of amateur and professional archeologists all over the world. Try a Google search for your state or province's archeological society. For example, I just searched for Nebraska Archeological Society (I picked Nebraska at random) and found a Web site belonging to a group formed in 2004. Bingo!

Closest college or university archeology department: Call them and describe what you found, tell them where your site is, and what peoples once populated the area. Since you took those pictures, offer to email a few over for inspection.

State historic preservation officer: Many states have a department that handles finds like these.

Don't get discouraged—it's possible that you won't get any interest from all of these parties. Or they may see your photo and dismiss it as a kid's former fort or some other natural formation. Keep searching—there are millions of legends out there and tons of other sites beckoning to legend trippers everywhere.

If your site is of interest, I'm sure the Indiana Jones in you will want to dig. That's understood, and the good news is there are training programs available through some of these archeological groups. You don't need a Ph.D., just a passion for solving mysteries. I'll see you on the dig or dive, legend trippers!

Religious

Tripping

"The Devil went down to Georgia,
he was looking for a soul to steal
He was in a bind 'cause he was way behind:
he was willin' to make a deal."

—Charlie Daniels

NOTHING MAKES PEOPLE QUITE as uncomfortable as discussing politics or religion. I can promise to avoid half of those topics in this book, and one outta two ain't bad. We must talk about religion because all of us are exposed to belief systems. Even if you're a devout atheist, you still pass billboards touting churches and religious teachings, you see "In God We Trust," on the back of currency, and of course there are those who sit next to you on planes or mass transit or visit your home to try to convince you that your way is wrong and their way is right.

If you were raised in a religion, you will never fully escape that programming no matter how hard you try, and then there are people who fully embrace belief systems. No matter which category you fall under, I tell you not to worry. You can keep your beliefs, I'm in no position to try and change your views. But I do ask that you have an open mind and respect that some people hold differing religious or spiritual views than yours, and these folks hold those views as absolute truth. As sure is two and two is four, their beliefs are true to them.

Religious texts are full of supernatural miracles, raising the dead, the wrath of greater powers, and ghosts. Religious tripping will show you a side of people that you won't see unless you get into the trenches with them and ask them with earnest to explain.

Millions of people make pilgrimages to sacred sites because they want to walk where the legend walked. Muslims make a journey to Mecca in Saudi Arabia; Jews may go the Wailing Wall in Jerusalem; and Catholics might visit the Vatican. There's no end to how people of faith work to place tangible locations and items into the religion they're taught.

Part of the reason I began legend tripping so many years ago was because I had big questions: Are we alone in the universe? Is there life after death? Who created all of this? Through legend tripping I'm finding answers, but they're my own. I recognize they may not mean anything to someone else. All I can do is pass on what I learn.

Religious discussions stir something deep and primal in many people. So I remind you again: Bring your open mind. I'll be right there with you. Hold my hand; let's jump in.

A DEAL WITH THE DEVIL

SUCCESSFUL PEOPLE HAVE LONG had their detractors. "He got lucky," one might say, even though the accuser isn't privy to the years of hard work and dedication; "He must have made a deal with the devil," is a more inflammatory accusation. The point of either statement is that some prominent figure doesn't deserve to be where he is, and the only explanation is supernatural (or preternatural, for you demon fans).

The Devil, Satan, The Opposer, Mephistopheles, Old Scratch, Beelzebub, My Former Boss; he goes by many names, but the person we're referring to is the fallen angel from Judeo-Christian teachings. The Devil rules the underworld, or Hell, and has his minions, so the Bible says. For many, the Devil is the scapegoat for when they do something wrong (i.e., "The Devil made me do it"), for others he's the voice of constant temptation. The Devil, we're told, is in a constant struggle with God over the souls of men. And unlike God, you can make a deal with the Devil.

Ready to make a deal with Old Scratch?

This "Deal with the Devil" legend has been replayed countless times over history and is at the heart of a classic country song (thank you, Charlie Daniels), but many agree the tale got its start around 1587 in Germany with the tale of Faust.

The gist of the story goes like this: Faust has an insatiable thirst for knowledge. He only cares about the here and now, and so he makes a deal with the Devil. In exchange for his soul, Faust is granted knowledge and power. The moral of the story is that Faust has a great life, but then pays the price for all of eternity.

There likely was a Faust who died in Germany around 1540. Dr. Johann Georg Faust was an alchemist, astrologer, and wizard who had alluded to the Devil as a kind of crony in his work. As with many legends, there's some basis in fact in this tale. But the story has been told and retold so many times that some even doubt its origins now. We can debate the origin, but we can't debate that this legend is alive, well, and real today. How the story evolves from its earliest roots is of supreme interest to legend trippers.

I'm a guitar player and have been since I was 13 years old. I play for fun and mostly noodle around in my basement. My best friend since childhood, John, started playing guitar about the same time I did. Since we were teenagers I've watched him grow to become an incredible musician who now makes a full-time living with his music, while I'm still in my basement playing for the crickets who sneak in through my basement door.

This used to frustrate me, though now I've come to realize I chose a different path, and John never stopped playing guitar, while I could walk away for a few days at a time.

In that frustration of knowing there are people out there so much better at guitar than I am, I can't help but wonder if there's some magic formula to getting great quickly. In modern times, the most famous "Sold My Soul to the Devil" tale involves Delta Blues legend Robert Leroy Johnson.

Robert Leroy Johnson, 1911–1938.

Johnson was born in Hazlehurst, Mississippi, May 8, 1911, and was not widely known in his day. However, his influence can still be felt as other musical giants like Muddy Waters, The Rolling Stones, and Led Zeppelin all cite Johnson as an influence. Guitar God Eric Clapton called Johnson "the most important blues singer that ever lived."

In his early years, Johnson lived on a plantation in Mississippi and worked as a sharecropper with his family. In his teens, he played the harmonica and Jew's harp, but he begged local musicians to let him try their guitars when they weren't using them. Eventually Johnson acquired his own six-string and saw the instrument as his ticket to freedom. Of course he couldn't play that well in the beginning.

Johnson wasn't cut out for manual labor and set out from Robinsonville, Mississippi, in 1931, with his guitar in hand to make a living as a musician. And here's where the legend is born.

For the next two years, Johnson is more or less missing. We just don't know what he was doing, but we do know he wandered back in to Robinsonville in 1933 and could play the guitar like he was ringin' a bell. The songs he had written were rivaled only by his incredible guitar playing. Local musicians couldn't understand how someone could get *that* good in such a short period of time. Soon, musicians claimed that when John left Robinsonville two years earlier, he stopped at a rural crossroads and made a pact with the Devil. In exchange for his soul, the Devil taught Johnson the guitar.

Signing the "Devil's Book" is a Puritanical symbol of a pact with Satan. In Michael Pacher's 1483 painting, *Wolfgang und der Teufel* ("Saint Wolfgang and the Devil"), part of his "Fathers of the Church" altarpiece, he depicts the Devil attempting to lure Saint Wolfgang into a pact.

From 1933 until the end of his short life five years later, Robert Johnson toured around the United States mesmerizing audiences. He penned such blues staples as "Sweet Home Chicago" and "Cross Road Blues," and likely had more than a few jealous contemporaries who couldn't figure out how he did it.

In his lyrics, Johnson made more than a couple of Hoodoo references, which isn't surprising considering his upbringing. Hoodoo is a type of folk magic practiced by African-Americans in the Deep South. The practice was used to acquire skills from various deities. Johnson mentioned "hot foot powder" in "Hellhound on My Trail," and a "mojo bag," in "Little Queen of Spades." One doesn't have to stretch one's imagination far to think Johnson may have done more than just practice, practice, practice to become so great. Besides the 29 songs Johnson left behind, we know little about his life, but we do know there's no record of him ever acknowledging a deal with the Devil in any way.

The legend of Robert Johnson selling his soul to the Devil is so powerful that blues musician Tommy Johnson (no relation), who lived from 1896 to 1956, came right out and claimed he sold his soul to the Devil in exchange for his guitar chops. This bold claim added mystique to the persona for sure.

CAN WE REALLY MAKE A PACT WITH THE DEVIL?

MANY RELIGIOUS PEOPLE consider the Devil to be a real entity and force in our world. Legend tripping means you seek out learned opinions as often as you can. It means reaching out to people who can explain a different perspective to you. For help with the Christian perspective, I called a childhood friend, Dr. Dean Osuch, who is currently the Pastor of Outreach and Local Missions for Northshore Baptist Church in Bothell, Washington.

Dr. Osuch and I discussed the role of Satan in the Christian church today and his experiences with people who have made some kind of pact with the Devil. In his career as a minister, he said he's encountered five cases where people claimed to have made a deal with the Devil. Four of those claims occurred in Africa when he lived in that country doing mission work, and one claim happened in the United States. He believes three of the cases to be genuine, one definitely not, and one inconclusive.

Osuch said, "If you were to look at all the main-line denominations of Christianity and look at their doctrine, I'd say that 90% of Christian denominations believe that Satan is an actual being who is alive today."

When a person makes a claim to Osuch that he or a loved one has made some kind of pact with the Devil, Osuch says he begins to investigate. He asks why the person believes there's a pact, what this person has seen, what he was told. His job is to offer guidance, even if that guidance is toward counseling and not exorcism.

"Can deals be made with the Devil?" I asked.

"I always look back at the Scripture," Osuch said. "I try to find, are there examples of people selling their soul to Satan? And there's nothing in Scripture that really comes close to that. But there are people who have allowed Satan to take control of their lives over certain things. In my few experiences, it's not like somebody goes to Satan and has a face-to-face confrontation with him and writes out a contract, like, 'If you let me be a great musician I will give you my soul.' It's not that type of transaction. It's more about allowing Satan to influence your life."

As for teaching or preaching about Satan, Osuch says he believes there hasn't been much of a spike in devil discussions in church because preachers want the focus on God and not the Devil. He noted how Africans talked about demonic possession as if it were an everyday occurrence, and he's starting to see a similar attitude growing in America. Osuch says he has seen an increase in interest in demons and the Devil in the last 10 to 15 years. I asked him why.

"When Jesus walked this Earth throughout the Bible, he's casting out demons, putting them into swine, he's meeting demonic men, and he's casting out those demons," Osuch said. "There seemed to be heightened demonic activity when the Son of God was walking the earth. Some people believe the reason for the increase in demonic activity is perhaps because Jesus is coming back again."

Cults

CULTS FASCINATE ME TO NO END. As a person whose passion is legends and belief, I'm always curious how someone goes from being a well-rounded, educated individual to handing over all of his worldly possessions to a cult leader, cutting off his own testicles, and wearing white sneakers before committing suicide at just the right moment to ensure that he gets a seat on a spaceship riding behind a comet. This example, of course, is the Heaven's Gate cult. On March 26, 1997, 39 of its members took their own lives in a rented mansion in San Diego, California. But it's only one example. There are many others: The Branch Davidians of Waco, Texas, and Jonestown in Guyana, where 918 people took their own lives.

Though the Heaven's Gate reference above sounds somewhat ludicrous, summed up in such an over-simplified way, we need to remind ourselves that those 39 members mostly believed in what they were doing. They had purpose and faith. They believed their charismatic founder, Marshal Applewhite, and his teachings.

Though many might disagree with me on this, my definition of a cult is simple: numbers. A few of you in the woods dancing around a fire is a cult. Hundreds of thousands or even millions of you attending regular meetings is a religion. Labels make neither group right or wrong. We're just talking about perception here.

Like any good legend, cult members first heard a story, and they wanted to know more. The initial story rang true to the point where turning over their money, possessions, spouses, or anything else the leader asked for made sense at the time to the individual.

There is an inherent danger when story or legend replaces a person's grasp on reality. Story can become as addictive as any drug, so I say to use all of this in moderation.

When it comes to cults, the legend tripper in me turns armchair psychologist. I want to know what force takes a person from working a job, owning a home, and having a family to a suicide pact with peers. There's a breakdown going on in there.

Cults may be the darkest corner of the world of legends. If a legend tripper can shine even the smallest light into that corner to show the world a glimpse, maybe we can help some people along the way and learn more about the power of story and religious belief taken to extreme levels.

The Heaven's Gate Web site is still active today.

POWER OF PRAYER

FEW RELIGIOUS PEOPLE will argue against the power of prayer. They will claim it's effective, it works, and your deity will answer (even if the answer is sometimes "no"). I was raised Catholic, and growing up I can recall dozens of instances when my maternal grandmother would announce that she would say a novena for me. A novena, for you non-Catholic types, is a series of prayers said either nine times on a single day or daily for nine days. In my grandmother's case, her novenas involved saying the Rosary daily for nine days. We're talking a grand total of 53 Hail Marys, five Glory Be to the Fathers, and one Our Father every day!

Please don't think that I was some awful child always getting himself into the kind of trouble that required such religious devotion from a grandparent. I wasn't. My grandmother threw around novenas the way other grandparents throw around quarters or cookies. "You have a math test coming up next week?" my grandmother would ask. "I'll say a novena." From a young age I speculated that my grandmother was too liberal with her novenas, and I doubted God's concern with my math test. I figured there were bigger fish to fry, and if I were going to call for divine intervention, I'd save it for something really big, like college finals.

For the faithful, prayer is part of daily life. Whether Witch, Christian, Muslim, Jew, Hindu, or any number of other belief systems, the simple act of setting an intent, taking a quiet moment to meditate on that intent, and asking for help from an outside source helps get results for the individual.

Intent gives meaning to actions and results. Without intent, you are meandering. A stroll in the park is fine, but when it comes to legend tripping, your intent will give meaning to the results you find. You need to be looking if you're going to find.

We've heard stories of people who prayed themselves healthy from terminal illness. The faithful may call it a miracle, others may say it was mind over matter (which is still miraculous in my book), while disbelievers will call it a coincidence.

There are clinical studies available showing a difference in recovery times. But those are cold numbers and statistics. Actually interviewing people yourself is a story more powerful than any number.

LEGEND TRIPPING ASSIGNMENT

Interview a person of faith who is recuperating from surgery. Find out how many people are praying for his recovery. Join in with the prayers yourself. Find out how long the recovery takes and measure it against an average. Ask the patient the big questions: How many people are telling you they're praying for you? Do you pray for your own recovery? Do you feel a difference?

When the Saints Go Marching In

CATHOLICS HAVE MANY SAINTS. People are canonized by the Church for their good works and their miracles. So far there are over 10,000 named saints, and many have specialties.

Many people have a St. Christopher medal in their car because he is the patron saint of travelers. The story goes that one day Christopher was crossing a river when a child asked to be carried across. Christopher agreed but soon found that the child was unbelievably heavy. The legend says this was the Christ child, who carried the weight of the world on his shoulders, and Christopher managed to carry him across the river.

My St. Christopher medal, the patron saint of travelers (and legend trippers, too).

Catholics believe they can ask saints to intervene with God on their behalf. So Saint Christopher can help you arrive at your destination safely. People may not even know the legend behind him, but they know he can help, and everyone can use a little help now and then.

I recall a story my grandfather told me about one of his golfing buddies who was a Catholic priest. This priest usually wore his black shirt and white collar while driving, and he liked to speed. One day my grandfather was riding with the priest when they were pulled over by the police for speeding. Many officers have a tough time writing a ticket to a priest, and this cop was no different. But the officer did manage to deliver a stern warning that the priest could understand and my grandfather never forgot. The cop said, "Slow down, Father! Don't you know Saint Christopher gets out of the car as soon as you're going faster than 65 miles per hour?"

Though I don't consider myself much of a Catholic anymore, I still carry my St. Christopher medal with me when I travel—knowing he's with me offers comfort at 35,000 feet.

We See Mary Everywhere!

LIKE OTHER RELIGIOUS FIGURES, she has many names: The Madonna, Mother of God, Saint Mary, or The Blessed Virgin. Mary is a religious figure who continues to show up in windows, on toast, in the sky, and a myriad of other locations. She's a figure of hope and a supernatural reminder for the faithful that she's watching us and is here to offer support and guidance.

The Madonna depicted in a religious statue.

One of the most prominent modern-day Mary sightings is centered on the small Bosnian village of Medjugorje. The faithful believe Mary has been visiting regularly since June 24, 1981, to offer messages from God. The messages are given specifically to six people in the village: Ivan, Jakov, Marija, Mirjana, Vicka, and Ivanka (known as "visionaries"). Mary delivers both public messages and private messages. She's also promised to tell each of the visionaries 10 secrets—prophecy of events to come for the world in the near future, or secrets that pertain only to them personally. Some of the visionaries have already received all 10 secrets. Three others already have nine as of this writing. Could the end be nigh?

So far only one secret has been revealed to the public. According to the official Web site (www.medjugorje.org), Mary said she would leave a visible sign on the mountain where she first appeared. This sign would be supernatural in origin, indestructible, and clear to all. The message from Mary was, *This sign will be given for the atheists. You faithful already have signs, and you have become the sign for the atheists. You faithful must not wait for the sign before you convert; convert soon. This time is a time of grace for you. You can never thank God enough for His grace. The time is for deepening your faith and for your conversion. When the sign comes, it will be too late for many.*

Medjugorje in Bosnia today.

Some of the visionaries receive daily messages. Millions from around the globe have flocked to Medjugorje to try to have a religious experience. Though only six people actually get to see and/or experience Mary, many find solace in just standing where Mary is said to have stood. One argument the faithful have made is that they can't see the wind, but they can see its effects. And that's good enough for many. Spiritual experiences are rarely group events; they are deeply personal and resonate with individuals for various reasons.

For most of the world, Medjugorje is far away. We can't blame the faithful in other parts of the world for wanting a sign closer to home. Fortunately, Mary gets around.

Near where I live in the Boston, Massachusetts, area, there was a hospital that garnered a lot of attention in June 2003 for a certain window. A strange image formed in mildew between two panes of glass at Milton Hospital. The image drew hundreds of visitors per day to gaze at a third-floor window on Highland Street in an otherwise non-descript brick building. For many believers, the image was that of the Virgin Mary holding a baby Jesus.

The stained window in Milton, Massachusetts, that drew thousands of faithful.
Visitors left offerings of flowers below the window.
Photos by Ben Garvin.

I interviewed Cecelia Garvin, who has worked at Milton Hospital since 1992. She worked in Room 201, right next to 202—the room with the now-famous window. "The window was like that for years," Garvin said. "The seal between the two panes of glass broke and this image came up."

Garvin explained how Room 202 was converted into an eye exam room many years ago as the ophthalmology practice inside flourished and expanded. Instead of removing the window and closing it up, they simply built a new wall in front of it to seal off the outside light. So there is no way to access the window in Room 202 from the inside without tearing through a plaster wall. The window is made with double-paned glass, so once that seal broke, moisture seeped in. The mildew eventually formed into the shape that made it famous.

The ophthalmology practice in Room 202 was started by Dr. Joseph Michon. As his practice grew, Dr. Michon found himself leaving for weeks at a time to do mission work. By 1975, Michon left his practice entirely to devote his life to journeying to some of the poorest parts of the world to provide medical care with a traveling mission. Though the stain in the window appeared many years ago, it wasn't until recently that the image took on a seemingly familiar shape in Dr. Michon's former window.

Garvin said, "That summer someone came up and said, 'Oh my God, it looks like the Virgin Mary,' so someone must have gotten in touch with the media."

By June 12, 2003, local media began covering the window, and within days there was a flurry of activity. "There were tons of people coming to see it," Garvin said. "It does look like the Virgin Mary. It does. Is it something that's a miracle? I don't know."

The mob of people who came to see the window grew to such proportions that the hospital lowered a tarp over the window except for a few hours a day to allow for observing. Hospital officials were concerned with their ability to run a medical facility with so many people in the way. The tarp helped control the mob until one day a mighty wind (or the hand of God, to some believers) came and blew the tarp and its frame into the window and cracked a corner of it. Visitors were crushed and feared they would lose their sign from God forever… but the image persevered.

Today people still visit the window, but not in the numbers that they used to. Flowers are left at the site, others stop and pray, and the donation box that was once there has been removed because people kept stealing the money. Though the Catholic Church's official stand was that this was not a bona fide miracle, even local clergy shrug their shoulders when asked what it means. People will see what they want to see in that window in Milton, and if it gives some hope, that's something the hospital can live with.

Author Mark Garvey wrote a book called *Waiting for Mary* that chronicled his search for Mary and that of the many pilgrims he encountered while on his journey. What I like about his book is his objectivity, not only with his subject but with himself. Garvey is a legend tripper, though he likely never labeled himself as such. I have two questions for him:

▶ Why did you go looking for Mary?

▶ Why do you think so many others seek her out?

"It was something that had been in my psyche since childhood," Garvey said. "I was raised a Catholic in the '60s, and those stories are just a part of growing up Catholic. Not that every Catholic believes them, but they're there for consideration." Garvey's interest was rekindled in the 1990s when he covered a Mary sighting event in Cincinnati near where he lives. "I met so many interesting people talking about so many other events that were happening at the same time around the country, that it naturally seemed like an idea for a book and something I could explore pretty thoroughly."

Garvey set out on a trip that took him around the United States to muddy farm fields, cities, and small towns in between. He mentioned how persuasive some of the people he talked to were, how they were convinced they had seen something religiously profound. Did Garvey think he might see Mary, or was he just an objective reporter? "I think that element of curiosity was there for sure," he said. "These people made some astounding claims. And you see some pictures that are obviously either faked or miraculous."

Pictures are tangible evidence for some people that back up their supernatural claims. Garvey described how people showed him photographs they had taken using disposable cameras. The pilgrim would point his camera directly at the sun and take a picture. In the developed picture you'd see a golden rectangle that they believed to be the gate to heaven (and *not* a cheap camera's shutter overwhelmed with light). In other pictures, Garvey saw religious figures, like Mary floating in the sky. "They were either faked or miraculous," he said.

Many make order out of chaos, and they find vision in the seemingly random.
I see a cheeseburger in the clouds… mmmm, cheeseburger.

Considering that the vast majority of Christians don't make these pilgrimages to sites where Mary (or other religious apparitions) is said to show herself, it makes one wonder if the few who do go are weak in their faith. If going to church is not enough, do they require physical evidence? Garvey said, "People approach spiritual things in a variety of ways, and I think people involved in this movement, their faith seems to be bolstered by these kind of events in which heaven is reaching down and taking part in our world in sort of a tangible way. It's just a matter of personality and what people need or expect from their faith."

Garvey is clear that he doesn't believe these sightings to be genuine events in which heaven is coming down, though he recognizes the believers have no doubt these are religious events.

Part of religious tripping involves testing, bolstering, and confirming your faith. Faith untested is blind faith.

Garvey noted that these religious figure sightings tend to heat up during times of turmoil. During the "Red Scare" era of the 1950s and '60s, more sightings popped up. The theme of the messages from Mary during this time period often warned of the evils of Communism. "The sightings increased again in the mid-'90s, to some extent in response to the upcoming millennium," Garvey said.

Garvey noticed very few messages from Mary were comforting. He said, "They're often visions of apocalypse, end times, dwelling on God's anger and retribution about to take place, that kind of thing."

So why would someone want to trek out to hear these doom and gloom messages? "I think they're getting some inner solace from imagining themselves being on the right side of cosmic history," Garvey said.

You will be surprised at just how accessible many authors and researchers are when it comes to your pursuit of legends. So many have Web sites, MySpace, Facebook, and/or Twitter that tracking down the experts is relatively easy. Getting them to answer your questions can also be easy if you hone your approach.

If you're going to send an email to an expert, be formal, be professional, be respectful, and be very specific. I've been on the receiving end of many an email question, and I will always ignore emails that look like this:

hey, how r u? LOL. So where can i find a gost near me?

But emails that are specific will usually illicit a response. Try something like this:

Dear Mr. Belanger:

I'm looking into a legend that appeared in one of your books. I live in Louisville, Kentucky, and want to know if the Waverly Hills Historical Society still allows overnight ghost tours?

—Thomas H. Hays

That email is short, to-the-point, and shows you're reaching out to me specifically because of something you read in one of my books, as opposed to firing off random emails to any paranormal person you can find. Email and the Internet are amazing, but what many people don't realize is because so many people are now so accessible, it's nearly impossible for some people to respond to all of the email they receive.

I Need a Miracle Every Day

"MIRACLE" IS A WORD that gets tossed around today. Like profanity, the overuse has diminished the power of the word. In sports, commentators and athletes often call wins "miracles." Just like saying someone sold their soul to the Devil in exchange for their talent, calling something a miracle also often undermines good old-fashioned hard work and talent. But when discussing religious endeavors, the "miracle" is an important concept. It's a required legend needed to keep a belief system growing and propagating.

Some events do seem truly miraculous. There have been people with terminal cancer or other life-threatening conditions that turned to religion, a faith healer, or a location where the sick are said to be healed, and they really have been healed, to the astonishment of doctors. Is this mind-over-matter or truly a miracle? For those who were terminally ill and the people who care for them, I'm sure they don't care.

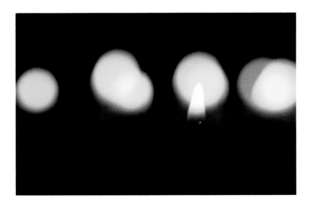

The idea of a religious healing miracle hits home for me because in May 1994 my mother went with her best friend, Pat and Pat's uncle, Rev. John Morley, a Catholic Priest, to Lourdes, France. Pat was 40 years old and terminally ill with cancer. She was past the point where doctors believed chemotherapy would help, and there was so much cancer that surgery wasn't an option. Pat needed a miracle. The more her health deteriorated, the more Pat looked to her Catholic faith for solace. Pat went to Lourdes intent on getting her miracle.

Pat was drawn to Lourdes because it's said to be a place for miracles. The town today boasts a population of about 15,000 people, though more than 5 million pilgrims come through each year. Located in the foothills of the Pyrenees Mountains, this small town may have been forgotten if not for a girl named Bernadette Soubirous, who, on February 11, 1858, encountered an apparition wearing a white veil, a blue girdle, and with a golden rose on each of her feet. This figure stood on a niche in the rock in the grotto of Massabielle. This apparition was experienced 18 times by Bernadette between February and July 16 of that year. Bernadette told others what she had seen and of the message: the need to pray more and make penance for your sins. On one visit, this figure told Bernadette to tell the priests a chapel was to be built in this location. The local priest was willing to listen, but he asked that this apparition first identify herself and then perform a miracle.

On the ninth visit, the apparition told Bernadette to drink from the spring that flowed under the rock (at the time, no one knew of a water source there) and to eat the plants that grew around the grotto. Bernadette said she only saw mud.

St. Bernadette.

She assumed the spring must be underground so she dug in her fingers, her hand came up with muddy water and she drank it and she ate the nearby plants. The gathered crowd was disappointed. But in the course of a few days, a spring began to flow there that still runs today. The crowd accepted this as the miracle they needed. The apparition must be Mary, and they must build a church there.

The town's people soon drank from the spring, and some believed it healed them of their afflictions. As of this writing, there have been 8,000 claims of miracles from bathing in or drinking the water of Lourdes. But only 67 were verified by the Lourdes Medical Bureau as having no other explanation.

Still, my mom's friend Pat believed she would be number 68. In May 1994, they headed to France. Pat was weak, wheelchair-bound, but determined.

When legend tripping, sometimes you'd love to get those exclusive interviews with famous people who had a brush with the unexplained. And sometimes you only need to look as far as your own family.

Here's my exclusive interview with my mom:

They took her in first. Now everybody's speaking French, and you don't know what's behind the curtain when they're administering to her. She couldn't stand or walk in by herself, so there were like six people, and they told me to help get her undressed, but they're telling me in French (laughs). So they take her through the curtain, and Pat never complained, never cried, never moaned, never did anything. All of a sudden I hear this blood-curdling scream. I went, "Oh my God, she's cured!" So then they bring her back in from there and she looks and me and says, "You're next." I said, "Pat, I don't have to go in, there's a million people around." She said, "You're going in."

I said, "Pat, no." She said, "You're. Going. In."

So then they started telling me to go in, I said, "Me no hurt. Me no need. Me good!" Yeah, hello, thinking they're gonna understand that. So then I get through the curtain and I'm standing at the top of the step, and it's a stone tub. Two steps in. And they're saying, "Okay, get in," and I'm saying, "No no, I don't need it," and I'm shaking my hands. They said, "Oh yes, go in."

It's the coldest my feet have ever been in my entire life. I said the longer it takes me, the longer people have to wait who want to really get in, so I go in the middle of the tub and the water's up to my knees. Now they're telling me in French to get all the way in. And I'm saying, "Nothing hurts!" I touch my back, my heart, I'm good. Then they're putting their hands in...get in...so I got in (laughs).

And when I went back, I saw Pat, and she said, "Got ya!" (laughs).

How did you feel when you went in?

Cold. But you know what, when I came home I really felt different from that. I really did. It was really amazing.

Pat passed away three weeks after returning home from Lourdes. One would guess she didn't get her miracle. Mom said, "You know people say that, but maybe she did."

THE HOLY GRAIL

LONG BEFORE MONTY PYTHON'S infamous and farcical quest for the cup or dish used by Jesus Christ at the Last Supper, there were famous quests to find this receptacle said to hold supernatural powers for those who drink from it. The only problem is, no one knows where the grail is, if it ever existed, or if it's a metaphor for anyone who seeks out Jesus and his story. The quest for the Holy Grail is so omnipresent that it's been romanticized, fictionalized, parodied, and documented. For believers, it's the ultimate physical connection with Jesus Christ.

You know how many references to the Holy Grail are in the Bible? Zero. Nada. In fact, for more than a thousand years after the death of Jesus, no one seems to have any interest in the cup he may have used at his last meal. The legend dates back to the late twelfth century when the French writer Robert de Boron penned the poem, "Joseph d'Arimathe." In the poem, Joseph is visited by the apparition of Jesus and given the Holy Grail. Joseph then takes the Grail to Great Britain, where a bloodline of guardians was established to guard this magical cup. But somewhere along the way, the Grail is lost.

King Arthur and his Knights of the Roundtable stories renew the world's interest in the Holy Grail, but still the Grail remains missing. Some popular locations said to house the Grail today include Saint Mary of Valencia Cathedral in Spain, beneath Rosslyn Chapel in Scotland, and even a house in Maryland in the United States.

Obviously the Grail can't be in more than one location, and perhaps it's in none of these places. Perhaps it will remain a metaphor—a quest that millions go on, a quest that's more about the journey than the destination, one that forces the pilgrim to assume the reality of the destination, ponder the implications of what it means, and continually seek.

As a legend tripper, I completely understand. This is about the journey. We take our religion and beliefs with us, it's part of our baggage. We use religion to interpret and make sense of the stories and events that shake our natural world. In the quest for answers, when science fails us, we often turn to religion—a system chock full of its own legends and lore. If we can be objective and try to limit the influences of our own religious upbringing, there's no reason our legend tripping can't take us into churches, mosques, temples, synagogues, or to sites of religious significance…you may just find a miracle or two.

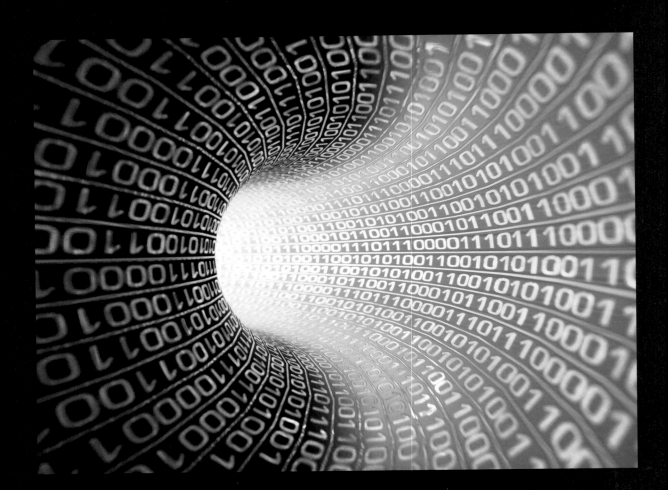

WEB TRIPPING

"The Internet is becoming the town square for the global village of tomorrow."

—Bill Gates

THOUGH LEGEND TRIPPING IS MOSTLY an active endeavor where you get out of your house and explore the physical (and maybe even metaphysical) world, thanks to the Internet, there are ways to trip even when you're rained in, snowed in, or just don't feel like heading out. You can go Web Tripping.

The World Wide Web is not only an invaluable research tool when it comes to choosing future subjects and targets for legend tripping, it's also become a legitimate world unto itself. Thanks to message boards, online communities, chat rooms, and video and audio chat applications such as Yahoo Instant Messenger and Skype, the Web has become a new form of reality for millions of people.

I have owned and operated a Web community called Ghostvillage.com since 1999. The Web site is designed for ghost trippers and those interested in the supernatural. I've been constantly amazed at how seriously members of our community take the world of our message boards. They care about their post count—because higher post counts mean higher member status; they care about being taken seriously by other members; and many vie for the position of "moderator," a kind of watchdog position that has functionality not available to regular members. There are people who visit our message boards every day. There are romantic couples who met online on our site and research groups that have formed after meeting in our corner of cyberspace.

The Ghostvillage.com message boards.

In a Web community, people can take on a persona. They can be outgoing when they're anything but at home. They can be tall, dark, and handsome, or brave and all knowing. The anonymity allows Web users to embrace online communities in a way that's very different from the brick-and-mortar world. The Web world is real in every sense for millions of people.

It should be no surprise that not everything goes as planned on the Web. There are legends being born in cyberspace that aren't too different from legends from your local cemeteries, old buildings, or near that military base.

One doesn't usually think of the Internet as a place for supernatural happenings, but maybe there's more to cyberspace than we previously thought.

THE WEB BOT PROJECT

IN 1997, CLIF HIGH and his associate George Ure developed a Web bot, or spider, to search the Internet. A spider is a relatively simple program that automatically browses millions of Web sites, "reading" them and looking for something specific. Search engines such as Google and Yahoo! use spiders to find new content on Web pages so their searches remain relevant. These search engine bots can automatically check in with Web sites at regular intervals and report back to a main database. If I post a new article or blog on my Web site today, the Google Bot will find this new information within a day or so, and that article will begin to show up in their searches.

So Clif High developed a bot that would scour the Web, looking for 300,000 keywords with emotional significance. When the bot found a "hit" on one of those words, it would record the word before and after it and report back to the central database. By performing this action on millions of Web sites and running the result through an algorithm, High found he could not only take a snapshot of the mood of our collective unconscious, but he found there were hints in the mood swings that foretold of problems. His objective for doing this was simple and pure—to predict movements in the stock market. If the snapshot seemed grim, then the general mood was bad, and an investor could pull his money out of stocks, wait for the market to take its dip from this bad mood, and then buy again at a lower price. The motivation was simple, but the reality grew more complex. Not only did the Web Bot Project seem to grab the mood accurately, it was predicting future disasters—and sometimes it was right.

Halfpasthuman.com.

According to the company's Web site (www.halfpasthuman.com), the magic is in the interpretation of data. The site says, "We employ a technique based on radical linguistics to reduce extracts from readings of dynamic postings on the Internet into an archetypical database. With this database of archetypical language, we calculate the rate of change of the language. The forecasts of the future are derived from these calculations. Our calculations are based on a system of associations between words and numeric values for emotional responses from those words. These 'emotional impact indicators' are also of our own devising."

The Web Bot Project's earliest profound prediction came in June 2001. Based on the bot's results, it predicted that a significant global event would occur in the next 60 to 90 days, "an occurrence of such proportions that its effects would be felt worldwide." On September 11, 2001, the world witnessed that significant event in the destruction of the World Trade Center in New York, the attack on the Pentagon in Washington, DC, and the plane crash in western Pennsylvania that was clearly bound for a bigger target.

Granted, saying something big is going to occur in two or three months and have global effects may not be a stretch at any given point in time. A major earthquake or natural disaster can kill thousands and disrupt millions, a financial crash can leave tens of thousands jobless and then homeless—these types of events occur with grim regularity. Regardless, the Web Bot Project picked up on a change of mood on the Web and a context that hinted of something bad to come. For my money, I need something more specific than "big global problem" to believe. There have been other claimed successes:

- ▶ American Airlines Flight 587 crash in Queens, New York, on November 12, 2001
- ▶ Space Shuttle *Columbia* disaster on February 1, 2003
- ▶ Northeast Blackout of 2003
- ▶ The Indian Ocean earthquake and tsunami of 2004
- ▶ Hurricane Katrina

There have also been misses. Ask any meteorologist: When predicting the future, things can get cloudy. In October 2008, the Web Bot predicted an event bigger than September 11 as far as world impact. December 12, 2008, a major earthquake in the Pacific Northwest was predicted, and they predicted a complete collapse of the dollar beginning in 2009 (okay, as of this writing, that one is still possible).

The company Web site can't stress enough that these predictions are for entertainment purposes and are only as good as the interpretation of the data, but the more interesting discussion here is this: Did High and Ure figure out a way to tap into the collective unconsciousness via the Web? And could that collective unconsciousness give us a glimpse of the future? The answer is a resounding *maybe*.

Swiss psychiatrist Carl Jung.

What is the collective unconscious? This is a term first coined by Swiss psychiatrist Carl Jung in the 1950s. To oversimplify the theory, in your brain you have your memories and life experiences. That part is obvious, but Jung also believed that we have some memory and experience with everything. Picture a universal thought wave that every human on the planet taps into. Within this collective unconscious are archetypes —personas that every person can relate to no matter where he lives or his social standing. Examples are these:

- ► The Self: our impression of who we are as an individual
- ► The Shadow
- ► The Anima: the feminine image in a man's psyche
- ► The Animus: the masculine image in a woman's psyche
- ► The Persona: related to the ego; how we present to the world
- ► The Child
- ► The Hero
- ► The Great Mother
- ► The Wise Old Man/Sage
- ► The Trickster
- ► The Devil
- ► The Scarecrow
- ► The Mentor

These archetypes, along with the collective unconscious, speak to all people. It's the collective human experience that floats around us like a morning fog. Imagine if we were able to tap into the collective experiences of everyone?

We'd make better decisions and be more prepared for what might come our way. If animals can sense danger, why can't we? If birds sense a drastic drop in pressure and know that severe weather is about to strike, why can't we? The collective unconscious is out there. Call it genetic imprinting if you wish, but there is something universal about the human experience. There's something about these legends that speaks to us on a primal level.

The Web *is* a good representation of our collective unconsciousness. Millions of people are blogging, Tweeting, and posting about everything from the mundane to the way they feel about big events. News sources post articles they believe readers want to see, and users "buzz" about those articles on various other Web sites, raising the profile of those articles. Figure out a way to take a broad snapshot of all of that human activity, and you will get a map—just as the meteorologist has a map based on satellite images and on-the-ground readings around the world. Learn how that data moves, and you may just be able to predict the future.

Now on to the bigger question: Can we predict the future either as an individual or collectively? The answer: Definitely. This example may sound like a joke, but I'm serious. Go out with your friends one night and try staying out all night when you told your roommate, partner, or spouse that you'd be in by 10:00. Oh… and don't call to check in or anything. Would you be able to predict that you'll be in hot water upon your return? Of course! But we're talking about something bigger here: precognition.

In 1993, Dean Radin, PhD, a Senior Scientist at the Institute of Noetic Sciences, developed a double-blind experiment to test precognition. He hooked his test subjects up using skin-conductance measures and a photoplethysmograph for fingertip blood volume (something that can test blood flow and thus arousal) and then showed the subject a series of randomized pictures on a computer screen. Some pictures might be neutral and calm, such as a beach scene, and others might be erotic or violent. What Radin discovered was that many of his subjects would have a measurable bump in arousal levels, sometimes two to three seconds before an emotionally charged image was shown.

If people are blogging, Tweeting, and writing articles based on their daily lives, perhaps some of the more precognitive-prone people are allowing information gleaned from the collective unconscious to sneak into their writing. Maybe there's such a thing as a global bad mood or good mood based around events that have yet to occur.

When legend tripping, part of what you're doing is feeling your way in the dark. Sometimes we can't quantify our gut instincts, but we know what we feel and see. To ignore those feelings would be inhuman.

Few will forget where they were and what they were doing on September 11, 2001.

I recall being in New York City about two weeks after September 11, 2001. The posters of the missing people were still plastered everywhere, and emergency workers covered in dust still roamed the streets as they took breaks from their exhausting work. There was a feeling that floated in those streets of Manhattan.

There was sadness, but also hope and unity. Unlike other trips I've taken to New York City before (and since), you could look at people as they passed by. You'd get a nod or two from others. The nod spoke volumes. "We're going to be okay," "I still believe in a better tomorrow," and even, "We're gonna get the bastards who did this."

There was emotion in the air, and if you read the writings of the day online or in the papers and magazines, there was emotion in the writing. Tapping into that emotion via a Web bot is genius. Being able to successfully interpret the results is magic, and the stuff of legends.

In studying folklore, I'm always looking for correlations. If I hear one interesting story from one person, I want to find two or three others who have no relationship to each other who have a similar tale. That tells me there's something more to this legend than just one person who is confused or making something up.

If nothing else, the Internet allows us to search for those other stories. Maybe someone shared something in a message board or posted a blog that allows us to make those connections. We can become our own Web bots on specific topics. With enough information, you *can* forecast anything.

Gleaning the future isn't the only paranormal happening on the Web. As I stated earlier, the Internet has become a real place with real characters.

John Titor aka Timetravel_0 Visits Us from the Future

In November 2000, a person with the screen name Timetravel_0 started posting messages on public Web sites. He claimed he was from the year 2036 and had travelled back to our time in a machine that is really like a car (though not a Delorean for you *Back to the Future* fans). He even posted pictures of his machine in some of his posts. He made vague references to future events, he took the time to answer almost every question posed to him in these message boards, and he entered into lively discussions and debates related to the plausibility of time travel. Soon, Timetravel_0 even revealed his real name: John Titor.

His first post in 2000 jumped right in: "I was just about to give up hope on anyone knowing who Tipler or Kerr was on this worldline. The basics for time travel start at CERN in about a year and end in 2034 with the first "time machine" built by GE. Too bad we can't post pictures or I'd show it to you."

CERN is the multinational organization responsible for building the Large Hadron Collider near Geneva, Switzerland. And GE… well, in the interest of full disclosure, I am a shareholder. I don't know whether to be comforted that they will develop a commercial time machine or to not believe it, considering how far their stock fell during the Great Recession of 2009… I mean if you had a time machine, wouldn't you go back and fix a few things? I digress.

Back to the legend of John Titor, the man from the future. At first, many figured this was a person enjoying the anonymity of the Web and simply role playing. Call it living out a geek fantasy. But Titor never broke character. He backed up everything he could with a consistent story.

He described the sensation of time travel:

> The gravity field generated by the unit overtakes you very quickly. You feel a tug toward the unit similar to rising quickly in an elevator, and it continues to rise based on the power setting the unit is working under. At 100% power, the constant pull of gravity can be as high as 2 Gs or more, depending on how close you are to the unit. There are no serious side effects, but I try to avoid eating before a flight.
>
> No bright flash of light is seen. Outside, the vehicle appears to accelerate as the light is bent around it. We have to wear sunglasses or close our eyes as this happens due to a short burst of ultraviolet radiation.
>
> Personally I think it looks like you're driving under a rainbow.

Titor said the machine travels approximately 10 years per hour. Given that he claimed to come from 2036, that's roughly a three-and-a-half-hour-drive back to the year 2000 where he first started posting.

Titor described a world war that took place in 2015 that killed nearly three billion people, but one that changed everything. Those who survived were brought closer together, people became family and then community focused, and the bigger picture.

Titor's biggest reason for coming back was to warn the world of a second United States Civil War that would begin in 2005. As of this writing, we are already several years past that year, but Titor would have a reason for the discrepancy. According to him, there are an infinite number of "worldlines," or parallel universes in which we exist, and there are different outcomes for each worldline. Following his argument, if you were to go back and find yourself as a baby and kill your baby self, you would not be undone. The reason is because every event from stepping on a bug to leaving a door ajar would create a new worldline with different outcomes. So for Titor to get home, he not only had to return to the correct year of 2034, he also had to return to the correct worldline or universe.

His objective seems to be to try and help our time avert this major war that changed everything. The only problem is (according to his logic), even if we avert the war, it only helps us in our worldline. His will have still gone through the war because apparently there's no way to change the past.

What about travel into the future? Titor also claims that is possible. The problem with that argument is greed. Sure there are altruistic people out there who might want to just take a joy ride a decade ahead, but if time travel is this accessible, someone will get greedy. He will want to know who is going to win the next Super Bowl so he can come back and bet, he'll want stock tips, he'll want to know what technologies and people to back. If the *Back to the Future* movie franchise taught us nothing, it's that to know the future is to control the world.

There is a Web site called www.johntitor.com that holds a vast collection of Titor's posts and pictures. It's entertaining to read what he described will happen in the coming years. His writing is articulate and cogent, he gives great details and model numbers, and he speaks of time travel as no big deal *when* he comes from.

Exploring time travel legends like this one allows us to explore paradoxes, to wonder what is possible when time and space are no longer a factor.

GHOSTS IN THE MACHINE

ANY WEB PROGRAMMER will tell you that sometimes things go wrong with applications. They work for a while, and though no factors seem to change, they cease working. Combine iffy programming with terabytes of chatter, Web posts, and other variables, and you get a picture of chaos. Making order from chaos is a basic human need. It's the reason we find shapes in the clouds and why we hear voices speaking to us in the wind whipping through dry autumn leaves. Our brains force the world around us into familiar patterns. But could there be other factors at work? Could an intelligent entity manipulate that chaos to form order?

In the world of supernatural research, there's a relatively new concept (from the late 1970s onward) of spirit communication using technology. The practice is called Instrumental Transcommunication or ITC. Any time you see a ghost hunter on television asking a spirit to manipulate lights on an EMF meter, you're watching someone practice ITC.

ITC is more spiritual than technical. By consistently focusing your intent on bridging the gap between the world of the living and the dead via a piece of technology such as a phone, radio, television, or computer, practitioners believe you can make contact. That means these devices aren't very different from traditional talking boards, better known by Hasbro's trademark name: Ouija.

Remember that board game, where you and some friends would place your hands lightly on the triangle-shaped Planchette, ask questions, and then the little table would slide around and give you answers? There are multiple versions of this available online. The figure below shows one from the Museum of Talking Boards.

I asked if this legend tripping book will be a hit. Woo-hoo!

Is this just random programming? Or can something otherworldly affect the outcome? The answer lies in the eye of the beholder.

If there's such a thing as ITC, and intelligent, interactive spirits can affect technology, then it would seem to follow that there could be ghosts in the machine. Perhaps haunted places aren't just cemeteries and old buildings; maybe they're also in cyberspace.

IT'S THE END OF THE WORLD AS WE KNOW IT, AND I FEEL FINE

I WAS ON GOOGLE, searching for forums where people claim to be ghosts/spirits of dead people communicating with the living. Specifically I search for "email from the dead" (in quotes). By using quotes around the phrase, Google searches for those specific words in that exact order. If I leave out the quotes, the words could be in any order anywhere on the page. I usually start with quotes if I think I have a good idea of what I'm looking for. The second result that came up in the search was a news item from the *Daily Telegraph* in England. The headline read: "Christian service 'sends email from the dead'." It was at this point I decided I could take a break from writing this book and read this very promising article.

When legend tripping, sometimes my attention deficit disorder (ADD) comes in handy…hey, wanna ride bikes? Sorry. So there I was reading about an online service that offers to send a pre-written email and attached files to up to 62 recipients after the rapture, when the few decent and just people are taken up to heaven right before Armageddon. What started as an online break from working on this book soon became a legend trip into religious lore right there in cyberspace!

The Web site in question launched in 2008 and can be found at www.youvebeenleftbehind.com.

TIP

When searching for phrases in search engines, start by putting the phrase in quotes. For example: "Most haunted place in Indiana," will yield different results than Most haunted place in Indiana. When you start searching, use longer specific phrases first.

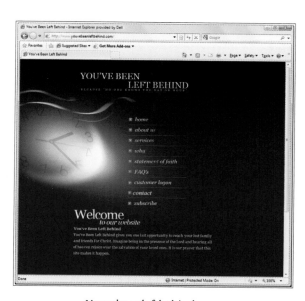

Youvebeenleftbehind.com

When exploring legends, you can't ignore religion. It's from religion that so many of these legends are born. Tales of devils, beasts, and monsters can be found in many religious texts. For those indoctrinated into a belief system, you grow up hearing about creatures and other tales of creation, healing, and supernatural magic. It becomes part of what you believe and is very difficult to set aside when you encounter a bizarre experience. It's the reason we devoted an entire chapter of this book to "Religious Tripping." So it would follow that people who hold certain beliefs will express them everywhere, including on the Web.

The more I read, the more I was intrigued. I must admit, at first I found myself scoffing at such a silly idea. I found my own beliefs creeping in to the fold. I found myself judging. Even after all of these years of legend tripping, I still find myself in those familiar pitfalls.

JUDGE NOT !

If you think you already know the answers to life's big questions, legend tripping isn't for you. Don't judge ideas or people. Don't assume you know all of the answers. You must accept that other people may have some insight and answers, or at the very least accept that others believe their position to be truth. When you're interviewing someone, be respectful and listen. Ask questions, challenge, but be fair. Attacking someone's beliefs will get you nowhere.

I found a contact email on the Web site and sent a note requesting an interview for this book project. I soon got a reply from the founder, Mark Heard, who said he would speak with me.

Before I interview someone, I always write down questions. This is just a road map; I'm always free to take side trips if the conversation goes in different directions. I write down questions because every journey needs a destination. We go into a lot more detail on this process in Chapter 7, "Interviewing the Witness."

Here are some of the questions I wrote down prior to my call with Mr. Heard:

What kinds of emails and documents are your customers trusting you with to send after the rapture? (*This question sounds open-ended, and it is. But why would people do this? If we're to believe the rapture is followed by Armageddon, isn't it too late already? Will we even have access to email when the skies fall and mountains crumble?*)

Why do you run this service? What's your motivation?

How can you ensure these emails will go out after the rapture?

How many people are signing up?

When Mark Heard answered the phone, I heard a tone in his voice. Here's how the conversation began when I called him at our appointed time:

Mark Heard: "Hello?"

Me: "Hi, Mr. Heard, this is Jeff Belanger, the author who emailed you regarding an interview. Is now an okay time to chat?"

Mark Heard: "Yeah, it's fine."

He had spoken only four words so far, but what I heard in his voice was a message. He was sizing me up. His words and slight sigh held one part trepidation, one part self-assured confidence, and a readiness to end this call with no notice. It was in those few seconds that a realization hit me. I'm sure he's spoken with other writers, and I'm sure more than a few have judged and ridiculed him for his beliefs and what he's doing. He has heard it all before. At that instant, I was humbled, and any judgments I had before were gone. It's not fair and won't help either of us. I told Mark I appreciated his time and I wanted to learn how he and his customers are expressing their spirituality on the Web. I figured my first question was both good and easy for him to answer. I asked what kind of content people were leaving for those who had been left behind.

"I would hope that people aren't leaving 'I told you so letters'," said Mark Heard, founder of Youvebeenleftbehind.com.

I laughed. Genuinely. "That's exactly what I was wondering!" I told him. Then he laughed. From that point on, I knew we'd be fine. The walls were down. He wasn't telling me to repent, and I wasn't telling him he's nuts. Just two people talking.

Heard explained that he believes those who are Christian and have a relationship with Jesus Christ will instantly disappear when the rapture comes. He estimates millions will be gone in a flash—the kind of thing that's sure to make breaking news. The rest of the world will be wondering why and how so many people disappeared. First, these emails will explain what happened.

Then, there's the question of what one researcher (me) calls the "nyah nyah nyah effect." If Armageddon is nigh, is it too late already?

Heard believes it's not too late. He explained that's where a post-rapture email message to non-believers can have an impact. He said, "If I and all of these other people are missing, then this is what happened and this is what's going to happen. There's still time for you to receive Christ and live with us in eternity.

"What gives me the basis for that is the [Bible] talks about he, the Antichrist, will be given the power to overcome them; that is, to martyr Christians who are here on the earth. There wouldn't be any if all of us were in the rapture and nobody gave their life to Christ after that. I do believe that there will be a short window, and the more opportunity that a person has had and the more teaching a person has had, then the shorter the window."

Here's how it works. Heard has four "saved" couples sprinkled around the United States, plus one alternate. This team of people is each required to log in to the system every day. He chose couples so that if one is injured, killed, or sick, the other can report in. If three out of four fail to log in for three days, the system figures the rapture has taken place. For the next three days, the system will email notices to all of the team members, warning them that they must log in to prevent the sending of the documents. If those three days go by with no log-in, the system sends its documents and emails out. Each subscriber receives several hundred megabytes in storage. Heard explained that users may use that space for photos or other documents that they want sent to up to 62 email recipients after the rapture.

I asked how many people were currently paying the yearly subscription, and he said, "Less than a thousand and more than a hundred."

Heard is not a preacher, and this isn't his day job. He explained that he's a church-going man who saw a need for a service. He sees his Web site as a way to evangelize what he believes in. The more we talked, the more my views evolved. I realized that if one is to have a belief system, you need to respect those who see it all the way through. Though I don't necessarily agree with that belief system, I now know where he's coming from.

My final thought was this: If millions of people do go missing overnight, and we quickly figure out they were all Christians, I bet it's pretty darn easy to "Come to Jesus" at that point. Even Thomas doubted; maybe that's why Mark Heard built his Web site.

MORE GHOSTS IN THE MACHINE

BACK TO MY SEARCH FOR GHOSTS in the machine. This time I narrowed my search for legends of spirits allegedly using technology to contact the living. I searched for cell phone calls from beyond (no quotes). I recognized the fourth result immediately as a page from one of my Web sites, Ghostvillage.com. Over the years, the site has published many hundreds of personal encounters from people who believe they've seen or been in contact with a ghost. On January 18, 2008, Ghostvillage.com published the following account from Jenna Gomes of Simsbury, Connecticut, who said these events occurred between 2004 and 2007.

When searching for cell phone calls from beyond, I also saw a link to an article on the popular Snopes.com site. Any legend tripper worth his salt should know and use Snopes. Considering the rumors, tall tales, and misinformation that fly around the Web like a swarm of gnats, it's good to have a reliable source that can debunk or verify some of these stories.

The article in question was called "Calls from Beyond." The claim: "A man's cell phone placed calls to his loved ones after his demise." The status: True.

When I was younger, my cousin Felix was killed while serving in Iraq. Ever since then, strange things have happened at his mother's house. The first events started one night at a get-together. All of Felix's friends, my aunt, and my sister were sharing stories of him when he was little. A beer can that was sitting in the middle of the counter next to them, with no warning, flew off it. Not rolled, flew. Like in the air. They all started laughing at that point...

...My cousin's old cell phone was kept in his car. My aunt and uncle never used it, but just keep it in the holster. One time, my aunt and uncle came home from a restaurant to discover three messages on their answering machine. The first one was from a friend. The second one was a garbled male voice, with people in the background. The third one was near silence except for a small male voice that could barely be heard. They checked the caller ID and were shocked to find that the calls were from Felix's phone. They rushed out to the garage and checked the car, but the phone was in its place and still turned off.

The article goes on to discuss a train accident that occurred on September 12, 2008, at 4:22 p.m. in the San Fernando Valley of California. A commuter train collided head-on with a freight train, injuring 135 people (46 in critical condition), and killing 25. For 11 hours after the wreck, the cell phone of 49-year-old passenger Charles E. Peck made 35 phone calls to his fiancé, his son, brother, stepmother, and his sister. When the family answered, they heard only static. When they tried to call back, the phone went right to voicemail. The family had heard about the crash and knew Peck was missing. The endless phone calls gave them hope that their loved one was in some debris waiting for rescue.

Emergency workers were able to use the cell phone signal to discover Peck's body 12 hours after the accident and one hour after the final phone call was made from his cell phone. Medical examiners determined that Peck died on impact. There was no way he could have survived for hours to make those phone calls.

Could this be a cell phone shorting out in a unique way or was this the spirit of a man attempting to say his goodbyes? We'll never know. As a legend tripper, you have to make peace with that outcome. You may never know. Exploring these legends may lead to more questions than answers. And sometimes you simply have to decide for yourself and let that be good enough. It's the journey, not the destination. But add up legend after legend and you have a bigger picture, a more complete story.

TOO GOOD TO BE TRUE EMAIL

IT'S A BLURRY LINE BETWEEN LEGEND and scam sometimes, and nowhere is that more obvious than the too-good-to-be-true emails we all seem to get. There are no Nigerians who need your help getting $20 million dollars out of the country—that's a kidnapping scam. And then there are the many emails that come in from major financial institutions like PayPal, or various national and local banks asking you to log in because there's a problem with your account.

That's called a "phishing" scam, where the email tries to lure you to a Web site that may look like your bank, but when you try to log in, you just handed over your username and password (and maybe even more information) to people who are about to rob you.

The email legends that I'm talking about offer luck with love, sex, or careers, or maybe even cash if you forward it to enough people. Here's one that hit my inbox recently that has all of the elements of a great legend. Check it out. (Many grammatical and punctuation mistakes remain intact.)

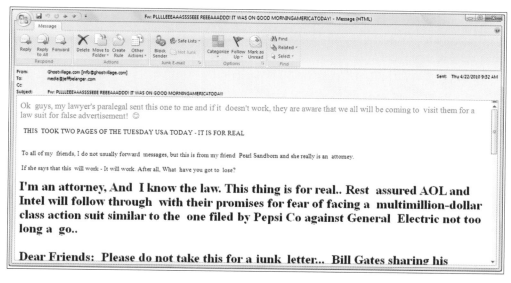

If it's in my email, it must be true!

Ok guys, my lawyer's paralegal sent this one to me and if it doesn't work, they are aware that we all will be coming to visit them for a law suit for false advertisement!

THIS TOOK TWO PAGES OF THE TUESDAY *USA TODAY*—IT IS FOR REAL

To all of my friends, I do not usually forward messages, but this is from my friend Pearl Sandborn and she really is an attorney. If she says that this will work—it will work. After all, What have you got to lose?

I'm an attorney, And I know the law. This thing is for real. Rest assured AOL and Intel will follow through with their promises for fear of facing a multimillion-dollar class action suit similar to the one filed by Pepsi Co against General Electric not too long ago.

Dear Friends: Please do not take this for a junk letter... Bill Gates sharing his fortune. If you ignore this, You will repent later. Microsoft and AOL are now the largest Internet companies and in an effort to make sure that Internet Explorer remains the most widely used program, Microsoft and AOL are running an e-mail beta test.

When you forward this e-mail to friends, Microsoft can and will track it (If you are a Microsoft Windows user) for a two weeks time period. For every person that you forward this e-mail to, Microsoft will pay you $245.00 For every person that you sent it to that forwards it on, Microsoft will pay you $243.00 and for every third person that receives it, You will be paid $241.00. Within two weeks, Microsoft will contact you for your address and then send you a check.

Regards,
Charles S Bailey
General Manager Field Operations

[*Author's note: Telephone numbers were listed for Charles, as was his email address. The phone numbers weren't working numbers. I sent him an email requesting an interview, and I never did get a bounce on the email, nor did I receive a response.*]

Thought this was a scam myself, but two weeks after receiving this e-mail and forwarding it on. Microsoft contacted me for my address and within days, I received a check for $24,800.00. You need to respond before the beta testing is over. If anyone can afford this, Bill Gates is the man. It's all marketing expense to him. Please forward this to as many people as possible. You are bound to get at least $10,000.00. We're not going to help them out with their e-mail beta test without getting a little something for our time. My brother's girlfriend got in on this a few months ago. When I went to visit him for the Baylor/UT game, she showed me her check. It was for the sum of $4,324.44 and was stamped 'Paid In Full.'

This has every element of a great legend. There are specific names and places, there are even phone numbers and email addresses if you want to verify (I would speculate that 99% of people wouldn't bother to verify by calling or emailing), and there's the promise of easy money just for forwarding. Besides, what's the downside for you? About 30 seconds of work for thousands of potential dollars. "It's just a marketing expense." And there's testimony with specific numbers. If it is a scam, what's the motive?

What I didn't show you in the email above were the dozens of email addresses in the headers as this email was forwarded again and again. This email has been going around since at least 2006.

Spammers love emails like these because they get to harvest sometimes hundreds of addresses from a single email. But recipients also love these emails for the same reason they like to buy a lottery ticket—for an almost insignificant price, you get to dream of easy money solving all of your problems.

Because of the Internet, legends can travel and mutate faster than any other time in history. The Internet itself has become a place for some legends to exist. The Web is an opportunity to plan your next outdoor legend trip, but it's also a terrain with back alleys and dangerous destinations waiting to be explored by the objective and the brave.

Conclusion:
Getting Started

"All that we are is the result of what we have thought:
It is founded on our thoughts, it is made up of thoughts."

—The Dhammapada, Buddhist Scripture

W E'RE NEAR THE END OF OUR reading journey together, but hopefully it's only the beginning of your legend tripping adventure.

Let me remind you again of two important concepts. In fact, if you take away only these two concepts from this book, I will sleep the sleep of the just tonight.

▶ Legends are real, living, breathing entities.

▶ You can find them, appreciate them, and walk with them. You were born fully equipped to legend trip.

I'll be right there with you. You don't need to be part of a group (though you can go in that direction), you don't need a lot of money (a hike to an ancient mystery is often free), and there aren't gurus or alpha personalities to dictate how this is supposed to be done.

I've done my best to lay out how I go legend tripping. This is my passion. In fact, writing this book has caused me months of being glued to my desk to work on this, and as I type out these final pages, I can feel that legend tripping desire in me stirring. It's springtime here as I write this. Warmer days, rainy weather, maybe some intriguing footprints will turn up soon, and I'll be traipsing through the woods to find them.

As I search, I'll ask my own big questions, I'll come up with my own theories, and I'll be glad to swap legend tripping stories with you if we should run into each other one day.

As I stated earlier, I mainly avoided theories in this book because I think yours are as good as any others, but there is one concept I'd like to leave you with... the idea of a thoughtform.

TUL-PA

PERMIT ME TO GET PARANORMAL for a moment. Perhaps there's another explanation for these legends that walk, crawl, fly, or suddenly appear. I've always believed there is more to any story, and in the case of legends, there's a catalyst, a seed that is sown based on a perceived inexplicable event. Sometimes the seed doesn't take root—there are millions of legends we've never heard of. Some grow into bushes—those wonderful but somewhat obscure legends that add color to our communities; and other seeds grow into towering redwoods—the biggies like Bigfoot, Resurrection Mary, Chupacabra, and the Loch Ness Monster. But what if our collective consciousness can bring some of these aliens, ghosts, and other assorted creatures into physical being? The idea may sound radical, but it's far from new.

If we look to Tibetan Buddhism, there is a tradition of the Tul-pa, or "thoughtform" as translated by anthropologist Walter Yeeling Evans-Wentz in 1927. In Evans-Wentz's book, *The Tibetan Book of the Dead*, he describes the yoga belief over bodily form:

Through transcendental direction of that subtle mental faculty, or psychic power, whereby all forms, animate and inanimate, including man's own form, are created, the human body can either be dissolved, and thereby be made invisible, by *yogically* inhibiting the faculty, or be made mentally imperceptible to others, and thus equally invisible to them, by changing the body's rate of vibration. When the mind inhibits emanation of its radio-activity, it ceases to be the source of mental stimuli to others, so that they become unconscious of the presence of an adept of the art, just as they are unconscious of invisible beings living in a rate of vibration unlike their own.

Inasmuch as the mind creates the world of appearances, it can create any particular object desired. The process consists of giving palpable being to a visualization, in very much the same manner as an architect gives concrete expression in three dimensions to his abstract concepts after first having given them expression in the two-dimensions of his blue-print. The Tibetans call the One Mind's concretized visualization the *Khorva* (*Hkhorva*), equivalent to the Sanskrit *Sangs ra*; that of an incarnate deity, like the Dalai or Tashi L ma, they call a *Tul-ku* (*Sprul-sku*), and that of a magician a *Tul-pa* (*Sprul-pa*), meaning a magically produced illusion or creation.

A master of yoga can dissolve a *Tul-pa* as readily as he can create it; and his own illusory human body, or *Tul-ku*, he can likewise dissolve, and thus outwit Death. Sometimes, by means of this magic, one human form can be amalgamated with another, as in the instance of the wife of Marpa, *guru* of Milarepa, who ended her life by incorporating herself in the body of Marpa.

According to Evans-Wentz, these master yogis can create thoughtforms the same way an architect takes an image from his head, to blueprint, to reality, and likewise they can destroy these forms. But what if they go undestroyed? And though Evans-Wentz implies that it's the yogis who have the power to wield at their will, wouldn't the rest of us also have the same ability, though without the focus and intent? If enough of us collectively believe in a *thing*, does that *thing* not become real in some capacity? Maybe it can even become physically real. I don't discount the possibility.

We often fall into the trap of thinking of a legend as a centuries-old story that has been passed down, filtered, and now bears very little resemblance to the original. Not always.

Now that you are developing an eye and ear for legend, you can spot the birth of new stories and accounts of the paranormal. You can find your own truth.

Legends are like art. They're designed to be interpreted by the viewer. Sure, the artist could tell you what it all means, but that's not the point. You see the sculpture, hear the song, view the painting, or read the poem, and you reach your own conclusions.

Here we are, my friends. The end of our time together, but this is just the beginning for you. Take this book with you if you need to revisit anything, or if you need some reassurance. I'm here for you. And I could think of no greater honor than signing your book one day for you. It's my dream that if you do bump into me somewhere and want this book signed that it will have mud stains, the edges will be well worn, and notes will be written throughout. Use this book, get it dirty!

If you just can't get enough, I invite you to get involved and share your own tales of adventure on my Web site: www.legendtripping.com.

All right, enough of this yackin'. Let's go legend tripping!

INDEX

License Agreement/Notice of Limited Warranty

By opening the sealed disc container in this book, you agree to the following terms and conditions. If, upon reading the following license agreement and notice of limited warranty, you cannot agree to the terms and conditions set forth, return the unused book with unopened disc to the place where you purchased it for a refund.

License:

The enclosed software is copyrighted by the copyright holder(s) indicated on the software disc. You are licensed to copy the software onto a single computer for use by a single user and to a backup disc. You may not reproduce, make copies, or distribute copies or rent or lease the software in whole or in part, except with written permission of the copyright holder(s). You may transfer the enclosed disc only together with this license, and only if you destroy all other copies of the software and the transferee agrees to the terms of the license. You may not decompile, reverse assemble, or reverse engineer the software.

Notice of Limited Warranty:

The enclosed disc is warranted by Course Technology to be free of physical defects in materials and workmanship for a period of sixty (60) days from end user's purchase of the book/disc combination. During the sixty-day term of the limited warranty, Course Technology will provide a replacement disc upon the return of a defective disc.

Limited Liability:

THE SOLE REMEDY FOR BREACH OF THIS LIMITED WARRANTY SHALL CONSIST ENTIRELY OF REPLACEMENT OF THE DEFECTIVE DISC. IN NO EVENT SHALL COURSE TECHNOLOGY OR THE AUTHOR BE LIABLE FOR ANY OTHER DAMAGES, INCLUDING LOSS OR CORRUPTION OF DATA, CHANGES IN THE FUNCTIONAL CHARACTERISTICS OF THE HARDWARE OR OPERATING SYSTEM, DELETERIOUS INTERACTION WITH OTHER SOFTWARE, OR ANY OTHER SPECIAL, INCIDENTAL, OR CONSEQUENTIAL DAMAGES THAT MAY ARISE, EVEN IF COURSE TECHNOLOGY AND/OR THE AUTHOR HAS PREVIOUSLY BEEN NOTIFIED THAT THE POSSIBILITY OF SUCH DAMAGES EXISTS.

Disclaimer of Warranties:

COURSE TECHNOLOGY AND THE AUTHOR SPECIFICALLY DISCLAIM ANY AND ALL OTHER WARRANTIES, EITHER EXPRESS OR IMPLIED, INCLUDING WARRANTIES OF MERCHANTABILITY, SUITABILITY TO A PARTICULAR TASK OR PURPOSE, OR FREEDOM FROM ERRORS. SOME STATES DO NOT ALLOW FOR EXCLUSION OF IMPLIED WARRANTIES OR LIMITATION OF INCIDENTAL OR CONSEQUENTIAL DAMAGES, SO THESE LIMITATIONS MIGHT NOT APPLY TO YOU.

Other:

This Agreement is governed by the laws of the State of Massachusetts without regard to choice of law principles. The United Convention of Contracts for the International Sale of Goods is specifically disclaimed. This Agreement constitutes the entire agreement between you and Course Technology regarding use of the software.